BASIC / NOT BORING
SOCIAL STUDIES SKILLS

U.S. GOVERNMENT, ECONOMICS, & CITIZENSHIP

Grades 6–8+

Inventive Exercises to Sharpen Skills and Raise Achievement

Series Concept & Development
by Imogene Forte & Marjorie Frank
Exercises by Charlotte Poulos

Incentive Publications, Inc.
Nashville, Tennessee

About the cover:
Bound resist, or tie dye, is the most ancient known method of fabric surface design. The brilliance of the basic tie dye design on this cover reflects the possibilities that emerge from the mastery of basic skills.

Illustrated by Kathleen Bullock
Cover art by Mary Patricia Deprez, dba Tye Dye Mary®
Cover design by Marta Drayton, Joe Shibley, and W. Paul Nance
Edited by Jennifer E. Janke

ISBN 0-86530-434-3

PRINTED IN THE UNITED STATES OF AMERICA

TABLE OF CONTENTS

CELEBRATE BASIC SOCIAL STUDIES SKILLS

Basic does not mean boring! There certainly is nothing dull about . . .
- . . . designing job descriptions for presidents and other high-level officials
- . . . solving puzzles to figure out who's got which governmental powers
- . . . following giant footsteps to decide how a bill becomes a law
- . . . fooling around with fascinating government acronyms such as the CIA, FBI, DEQ, FCC, FDIC, BLM, BIA, NASA, IRS, FHA, INS, NFS, and the FTC
- . . . listening in on speeches about the government and deciding which ones are true
- . . . putting the Bill of Rights to work in real-life scenarios
- . . . showing off that you can tell a referendum from an initiative and a recession from a depression
- . . . matching sensational headlines with the presidents in office while they happened
- . . . solving the mystery of who's behind which door in the Cabinet

These are just some of the adventures students can explore as they celebrate basic social studies skills. The idea of celebrating the basics is just what it sounds like—enjoying and getting good at knowing about the government and economy of the United States. Each page invites learners to try a high-interest, appealing exercise that will strengthen or review one specific geography skill. This is no ordinary fill-in-the-blanks way to learn! These exercises are fun and surprising. Students follow a sassy American eagle, Egbert, their tour guide to the American government and economy, as they do the useful work of practicing social studies skills. They'll review intriguing, important facts about the structure of the government, the workings of the economy, and the rights and responsibilities of citizens right along with Egbert!

The pages in this book can be used in many ways:
- to sharpen or review a skill with one student
- to reinforce the skill with a small or large group
- by students working on their own
- by students working under the direction of a parent or teacher

Each page may be used to introduce a new skill, to reinforce a skill, or even to assess a student's performance of a skill. And, there's more than just the great student activities! You will also find an appendix of resources helpful for students and teachers—including a ready-to-use test for assessing government, economy, and citizenship facts and skills. Students will need access to social studies resources such as an almanac and U.S. history book. A copy of the U.S. Constitution is also recommended.

As your students take on the challenges of these adventures with the U.S. government and economy, they will grow. And as you watch them check off the basic social studies skills they've sharpened, you can celebrate with them!

The Skills Test (pages 56–59)
Use the skills test as a pretest and/or a post-test. This will help you check the students' mastery of basic social studies skills in the area of U.S. government, economics, and citizenship, and to prepare them for success on achievement tests.

SKILLS CHECKLIST FOR
U.S. GOVERNMENT, ECONOMICS, & CITIZENSHIP

✔	SKILL	PAGE(S)
	Review terms and concepts related to U.S. government and economics	10, 11, 50
	Recognize the key ideas of the Declaration of Independence	12
	Distinguish among important documents in U.S. history and government	12, 13
	Explore the contents and principles of the Constitution	13–18
	Recognize the contents and significance of the Bill of Rights	16, 17
	Recognize the significance of amendments to the Constitution; identify key amendments	18
	Explain the structure of the federal government and the concept of separation of powers	19
	Identify the duties, requirements, and officials of the executive branch	20–23
	Describe the members and functions of the president's cabinet	22
	Identify the names and functions of key government agencies	23
	Identify the duties, requirements, and officials of the legislative branch	24–29
	Identify the powers of Congress and the limits on its powers	27, 32
	Recognize the rights and responsibilities of state governments	27, 32
	Describe how laws are made	28, 29
	Identify the duties, requirements, and officials of the judicial branch	30, 31
	Recognize the significance of some key court decisions	31
	Identify examples of reserved powers, delegated powers, and concurrent powers	32
	Explain how presidents and other officials are elected	33–35
	Identify some U.S. presidents and events that took place during their administrations	36, 37
	Identify national symbols, traditions, and holidays and their significance	38, 39
	Identify key national landmarks	40, 41
	Identify current officials at the national, state and local levels	42
	Describe rights and responsibilities of citizens	43
	Identify ways citizens can participate in government	43
	Recognize some key citizens that made contributions to the United States	44, 45
	Recognize some of the workings of the U.S. economic system	46–49
	Identify some features of the relationship between money and the government	46
	Describe some of the uses of taxes	47
	Describe some economic principles and terms	48, 49

U.S. GOVERNMENT, ECONOMICS, & CITIZENSHIP

Skills Exercises

WHERE WOULD YOU FIND IT?

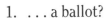

Get started on a tour of the United States government and economic systems. This friendly American Eagle, Egbert, has offered to be your guide, since he knows a lot about this topic.

These are some of the things you'll run across on your tour. Where (on your tour of the government and economy) do you think you'll find each of them?

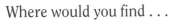

Where would you find . . .

1. . . . a ballot?
   a. in a bank
   b. in an election
   c. near a statue
   d. in a parade

2. . . . a quorum?
   a. on the President's desk
   b. beside the Washington Monument
   c. in the House of Representatives
   d. in the Declaration of Independence

3. . . . a stock?
   a. in a portfolio
   b. in a salad
   c. in the Constitution
   d. in a ballot box

4. . . . an entrepreneur?
   a. sitting on the Supreme Court
   b. running a business
   c. leading the U.S. Coast Guard
   d. robbing a pawnshop

5. . . . a Secretary of the Interior?
   a. at a bank
   b. running a decorating business
   c. at the Treasury Department
   d. in the President's Cabinet

6. . . . the Attorney General?
   a. at the Pentagon
   b. at the Justice Department
   c. at the U.S. mint
   d. at the Federal Reserve

7. . . . a habeas corpus?
   a. in a morgue
   b. in the Constitution
   c. in the Department of Transportation
   d. in the National Forest Service

8. . . . an Article?
   a. in the Preamble
   b. in the Declaration of Independence
   c. in the Department of Agriculture
   d. in the Constitution

9. . . . a senator?
   a. at the stock market
   b. in Congress
   c. at the Bureau of Engraving & Printing
   d. in the Department of Labor

10. . . . a suffragette?
    a. at the Federal Reserve
    b. at the Pentagon
    c. in a protest march
    d. at a Social Security office

Use with page 11.

Name

11. . . . an elastic clause?
   a. in a laundry
   b. at the Department of Education
   c. in the Constitution
   d. in an election

Wow! This Declaration is a great read!

12. . . . a branch?
   a. in the federal government
   b. at the Federal Reserve
   c. at the U.S. Treasury Department
   d. at a polling place

17. . . . a bill?
   a. in Congress
   b. in the Constitution
   c. in the Declaration of Independence
   d. in the Supreme Court

13. . . . the Commander-in-Chief?
   a. in the Senate
   b. at the Pentagon
   c. in the White House
   d. in the Supreme Court

18. . . . a serial number?
   a. on the Bill of Rights
   b. on a ballot
   c. on a dollar bill
   d. on the Constitution

14. . . . millions of milled coins?
   a. at the U.S. mint
   b. at the Department of Labor
   c. in the President's Cabinet
   d. at the Central Intelligence Agency

19. . . . "We hold these truths to be self-evident,. . ."?
   a. in the Declaration of Independence
   b. in the Army
   c. in the Constitution
   d. in a stock portfolio

15. . . . a bond?
   a. on an Air Force bomber
   b. at the Department of Labor
   c. in a safe deposit box
   d. in a courthouse

20. . . . a preamble?
   a. on a $5 bill
   b. in the Senate
   c. at the beginning of the Constitution
   d. in a stock portfolio

16. . . . a veto?
   a. on a new $100 bill
   b. on a legislative bill
   c. on new a $1000 bill
   d. on a ballot

21. . . . some currency?
   a. in a bank
   b. in the Declaration of Independence
   c. at the Department of Energy
   d. at the National Parks Service

Use with page 10.

Name

IN THE COURSE OF HUMAN EVENTS...

What's so great about an old, old piece of paper? The Declaration of Independence—even though it is over 200 years old—is still the basis of American Democracy.

It declares the colonists' independence from Great Britain and lists the reasons for this action. The wording is old-fashioned, and hard to understand. Take a chance at figuring out what you think it means. The first part of the document is here. Read it, then answer the questions using your own, modern, everyday words. (Use a separate piece of paper.)

When, in the Course of human events, it becomes necessary for one people to dissolve the political bands which have connected them with another, and to assume, among the powers of the earth, the separate and equal station which the laws of nature and of nature's God entitle them, a decent respect to the opinions of mankind requires that they should declare the causes which impel them to the separation.

We hold these truths to be self-evident, that all men are created equal, that they are endowed by their Creator with certain unalienable Rights, that among these are Life, Liberty, and the pursuit of Happiness.

That, to secure these rights, Governments are instituted among Men, deriving their just powers from the consent of the governed.

That, whenever any Form of Government becomes destructive of these ends, it is the Right of the People to alter or to abolish it, and to institute new Government, laying its foundation on such principles, and organizing its powers in such form, as to them shall seem most likely to effect their Safety and Happiness.

1. In the first paragraph, who are "one people"?
2. What does "dissolve the political bands" mean?
3. What words tell why the colonists are telling the reasons for declaring their Independence?
4. What do you think the authors meant by ". . . that all men are created equal"?
5. "Unalienable rights" has nothing to do with aliens from space, but what does it mean?
6. What natural rights does the declaration say that we are entitled to?
7. According to the third paragraph, what are governments made to do?
8. Who gives governments "just" powers?
9. In the fourth paragraph, what is "the right of the people"?
10. When must people use that right?

Name

WHICH PART IS WHICH?

Do you get the parts of the Constitution confused? Here's a chance to get them untangled! The Constitution is made up of different parts, which often get talked about as separate documents: the Preamble, the Articles, the Bill of Rights, and the Amendments.

Unscramble the mixed-up descriptions of the parts of the Constitution. Color each title for a part of the Constitution with a different color. Then color the phrases that describe that part with the matching color.

Similar to beliefs of the Iroquois League of Nations

First 3 deal with the separate branches of the government

These change the *Constitution*

These provide protection for citizens' basic rights and freedoms

More can be added to the *Constitution*

The Final Section of the *Constitution*

Made up of first ten amendments to the *Constitution*

We the people of the United States, in order to form a more perfect Union, establish justice, insure domestic tranquillity, provide for the common defense, promote the general welfare, and secure the blessing of liberty to ourselves and our posterity, do ordain and establish this Constitution for the United States of America.

Last 4 discuss the powers of the states and procedures for amending the *Constitution*

Bill of Rights

In the beginning, the states insisted that this be added to the *Constitution*

The Introduction to the *Constitution*

Presently, there are 27

Preamble

The main body of the *Constitution*

ONLY 52 words long

The first one protects freedom of speech, thought, and belief

Articles

Amendments

Name

CONSTITUTION SEARCH

Get to know your way around the United States *Constitution*. Egbert will serve as your tour guide, but you will need a copy of the *Constitution* too. It's your job to figure out which part of the *Constitution* applies to different situations.

Read each one of Egbert's wind-blown notes about the *Constitution*. Decide which part of the *Constitution* contains law that allows that situation to be the way it is. Write **P** (for *Preamble*), **A** (for *Articles*), **B** (for *Bill of Rights*), or **AM** (for *Amendments* 11–27).

5. _____
A 40-year old man, who was born in the United States, announces his decision to run for President.

1. _____
A 35-year old woman from Idaho is running for a seat in the House of Representatives. She immigrated to the United States 15 years ago, and became a U.S. citizen 6 years later.

6. _____
A senator did not like a ruling made by one of the Supreme Court justices. This senator cannot write a bill that would reduce the judge's salary or remove her job.

2. _____
We live in a country that assures justice for all, and freedom for ourselves and future Americans.

7. _____
The states of Oregon and Washington could become one state only if both state legislatures and Congress approve of the formation of the new state.

3. _____
Congress can't ask a citizen of Oregon to pay more federal taxes than his cousin does who lives in Indiana.

4. _____
In this country, the police must have a search warrant to search your home.

8. _____
It is the job of the executive branch of the U.S. government to make sure citizens obey the law.

Use with page 15.

Name _____

Basic Skills/U.S. Government, Economics, & Citizenship 6-8+

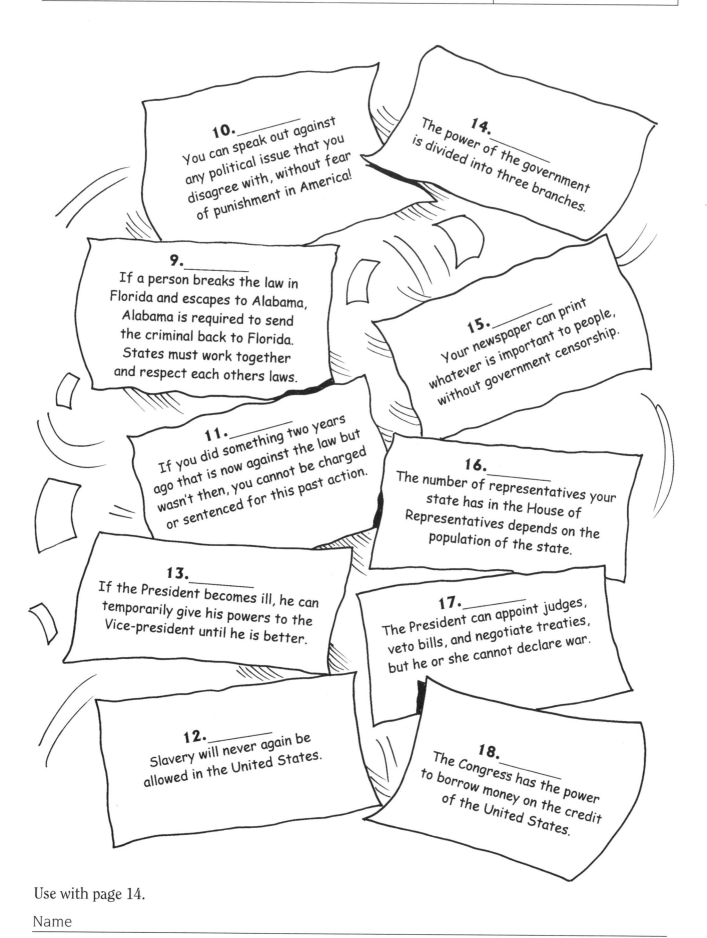

10. _____ You can speak out against any political issue that you disagree with, without fear of punishment in America!

14. _____ The power of the government is divided into three branches.

9. _____ If a person breaks the law in Florida and escapes to Alabama, Alabama is required to send the criminal back to Florida. States must work together and respect each others laws.

15. _____ Your newspaper can print whatever is important to people, without government censorship.

11. _____ If you did something two years ago that is now against the law but wasn't then, you cannot be charged or sentenced for this past action.

16. _____ The number of representatives your state has in the House of Representatives depends on the population of the state.

13. _____ If the President becomes ill, he can temporarily give his powers to the Vice-president until he is better.

17. _____ The President can appoint judges, veto bills, and negotiate treaties, but he or she cannot declare war.

12. _____ Slavery will never again be allowed in the United States.

18. _____ The Congress has the power to borrow money on the credit of the United States.

Use with page 14.

Name _____

KNOW YOUR RIGHTS!

The Bill of Rights is not an ordinary bill. You don't have to pay it, like a bill in a restaurant. It is a bill that you get to keep; and that's a good thing because it gives citizens many protections and guarantees of freedoms. When the Constitution of the United States was written, the people of the new country insisted that a statement of these rights be added.

What are these rights? The speakers on this page and page 17 are describing some of these rights. Do you know what they are? Find a copy of the Bill of Rights (the first 10 amendments to the Constitution). Read this document.

Inside each "talk bubble," write the number of the amendment in which that right is described.

A. I cannot be searched without a good cause.

B. I am free to practice any religion I want.

C. If I am accused of a crime, I have a right to hear the witnesses against me.

D. If someone sues me for more than $20, I have a right to a trial by jury.

E. If I am accused of a crime, I have a right to a speedy public trial.

F. Powers not given to the U.S. by the Constitution belong to the states or to the people.

Use with page 17.

Name

G. Rights in the Constitution should not be used to deny other rights.

H. I can speak out against my government if I don't agree with something it does.

I. I have the right to speak or publish my thoughts and opinions freely.

J. If I am charged with a crime, I have a right to a defense by a lawyer.

K. I can't be held for a crime without a grand jury indictment.

L. I cannot be required to pay an excessive fine or amount of bail.

M. If the police want to search my home, they can't come in without a warrant from a judge.

N. I have the right to own and keep a gun.

O. In a criminal case, I cannot be required to give witness against myself.

Q. The government cannot require me to keep soldiers in my home...

P. I cannot be given cruel and unusual punishment if I am convicted of a crime.

...or nest!

Use with page 16.

Name

WHAT GIVES YOU THE RIGHT...?

What gives you the right to vote? What gives you the right to a fair income tax? What gives people their freedom? After the **Bill of Rights** became part of the *Constitution*, other changes in the *Constitution* were needed. Changes are made through amendments to the *Constitution*.

Which amendment makes each change? Write its number.

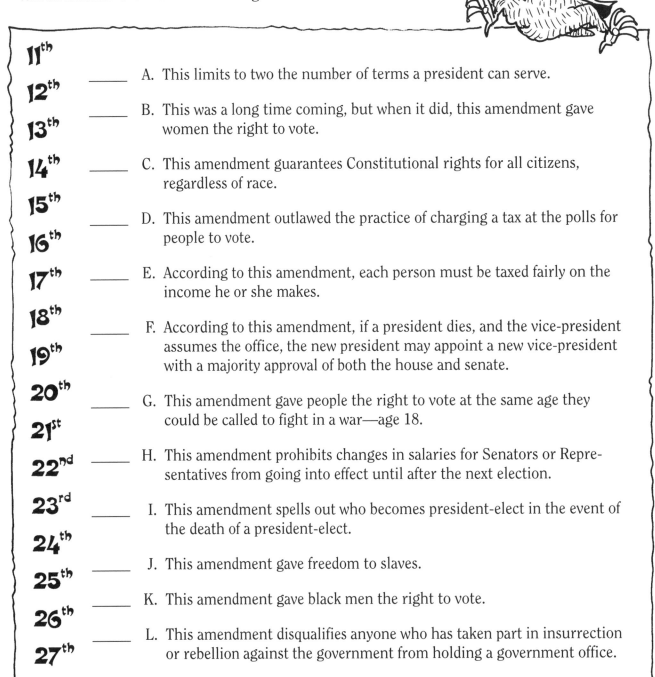

11th

12th _____ A. This limits to two the number of terms a president can serve.

13th _____ B. This was a long time coming, but when it did, this amendment gave women the right to vote.

14th _____ C. This amendment guarantees Constitutional rights for all citizens, regardless of race.

15th

16th _____ D. This amendment outlawed the practice of charging a tax at the polls for people to vote.

17th _____ E. According to this amendment, each person must be taxed fairly on the income he or she makes.

18th

19th _____ F. According to this amendment, if a president dies, and the vice-president assumes the office, the new president may appoint a new vice-president with a majority approval of both the house and senate.

20th _____ G. This amendment gave people the right to vote at the same age they could be called to fight in a war—age 18.

21st

22nd _____ H. This amendment prohibits changes in salaries for Senators or Representatives from going into effect until after the next election.

23rd _____ I. This amendment spells out who becomes president-elect in the event of the death of a president-elect.

24th

25th _____ J. This amendment gave freedom to slaves.

26th _____ K. This amendment gave black men the right to vote.

27th _____ L. This amendment disqualifies anyone who has taken part in insurrection or rebellion against the government from holding a government office.

Name _____

CHECKS & BALANCES

The U.S. government is like a tree. It has branches. This system is considered a wise and safe method of government, because it separates the powers so that no one branch holds total control. Each branch has a way to check or balance the power of the others.

Egbert drew the government tree to help you review the branches and separation of powers. Look at the chart, review your knowledge of facts about the government, then follow the directions below.

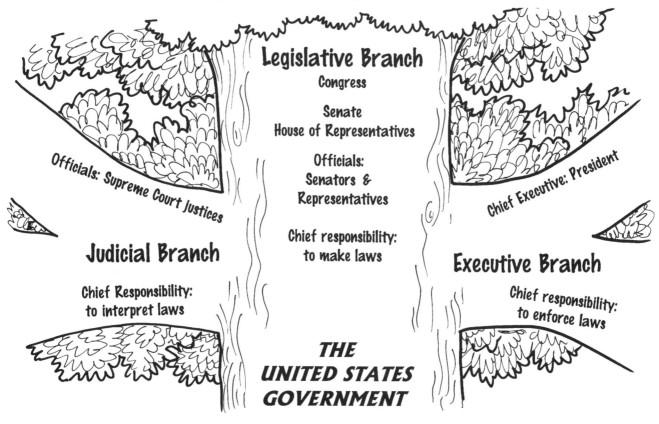

Officials: Supreme Court Justices

Legislative Branch

Congress

Senate
House of Representatives

Officials:
Senators &
Representatives

Chief responsibility:
to make laws

Chief Executive: President

Judicial Branch

Chief Responsibility:
to interpret laws

Executive Branch

Chief responsibility:
to enforce laws

**THE
UNITED STATES
GOVERNMENT**

1. Draw a black arrow from the branch that is Commander-in-Chief of the armed forces to the branch that controls funds necessary to maintain the armed forces.
2. Circle in black the title of the only branch that can declare war.
3. Use green to color the branch that passes laws.
4. Use red to color the branch that interprets laws.
5. Use brown to color the branch that enforces laws.
6. Draw a red arrow from the branch that can veto bills to the branch that can override a veto.
7. Draw a green arrow from the branch that can appoint judges and ambassadors to the part of a branch that can reject these appointments.

8. Draw a blue arrow from the branch that has the power to make treaties with foreign governments to the branch that gives the advice and consent for these treaties.
9. Circle in orange the title of the part of a branch that can bring charges against the president if he/she commits a serious crime.
10. Circle in yellow the title of the part of the branch that acts as jury in presidential impeachment proceedings.
11. Circle in purple the title of the branch that can impeach a Supreme Court justice.

Name

VIP JOB DESCRIPTIONS

Check out these advertisements for jobs! Did you know that the requirements to hold a high public job such as President, Senator, or Representative vary depending on the office? Read each notice below, and decide what the job is. Write the title of the office (the job title) on the poster for each job description.

What happens when the person who holds the highest job in the country cannot continue with the job? Tell who the next officials are that would take over the president's job.

SUCCESSION TO THE PRESIDENCY

1. _____

2. _____

3. _____

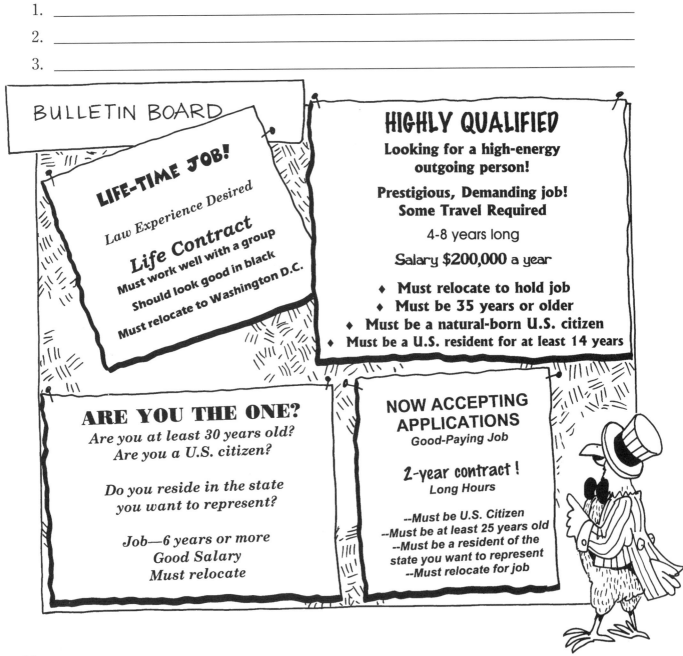

BULLETIN BOARD

LIFE-TIME JOB!
Law Experience Desired
Life Contract
Must work well with a group
Should look good in black
Must relocate to Washington D.C.

HIGHLY QUALIFIED
Looking for a high-energy outgoing person!

Prestigious, Demanding job! Some Travel Required

4-8 years long

Salary $200,000 a year

♦ **Must relocate to hold job**
♦ **Must be 35 years or older**
♦ **Must be a natural-born U.S. citizen**
♦ **Must be a U.S. resident for at least 14 years**

ARE YOU THE ONE?
Are you at least 30 years old?
Are you a U.S. citizen?

Do you reside in the state you want to represent?

Job—6 years or more
Good Salary
Must relocate

NOW ACCEPTING APPLICATIONS
Good-Paying Job

2-year contract !
Long Hours

--Must be U.S. Citizen
--Must be at least 25 years old
--Must be a resident of the state you want to represent
--Must relocate for job

Name _____

A HIGH-LEVEL JOB DESCRIPTION!

Being President is not an easy job. The Constitution describes many different presidential duties and responsibilities for the U.S. President. Only people with a lot of energy should apply for this job!

These descriptions for the President's various jobs are incomplete. Read the headings in these ads. Then write the description of the duties that fall under that heading.

A.

WANTED
EXTREMELY CAPABLE PERSON
TO BE **COMMANDER IN CHIEF...**

B.

WANTED
PERSON WITH A "TAKE CHARGE" ATTITUDE
TO HEAD UP THE COUNTRY
AS **CHIEF EXECUTIVE...**

C.

WANTED
INTERNATIONALLY SAVVY PERSON
TO BE **CHIEF OF STATE...**

D.

WANTED
CONSTITUTIONALLY AWARE SHARP THINKER
TO BE **CHIEF LEGISLATOR...**

E.

WANTED
STRONG LEADER & VISIONARY
TO BE **CHIEF OF THE PARTY...**

HELP WANTED DEPARTMENT

Some of these jobs sound pretty good!

Name

WHO'S BEHIND THAT DOOR?

There are a lot of closed doors down these hallways. Who works behind them? Each door enters a department of the Executive Branch of the U.S. Government. A Cabinet member is working behind each one. Most of them have the title of Secretary of their department.

Read the word or phrase on the door that describes the responsibility of the department. Then write the full job title that belongs on the name plate.

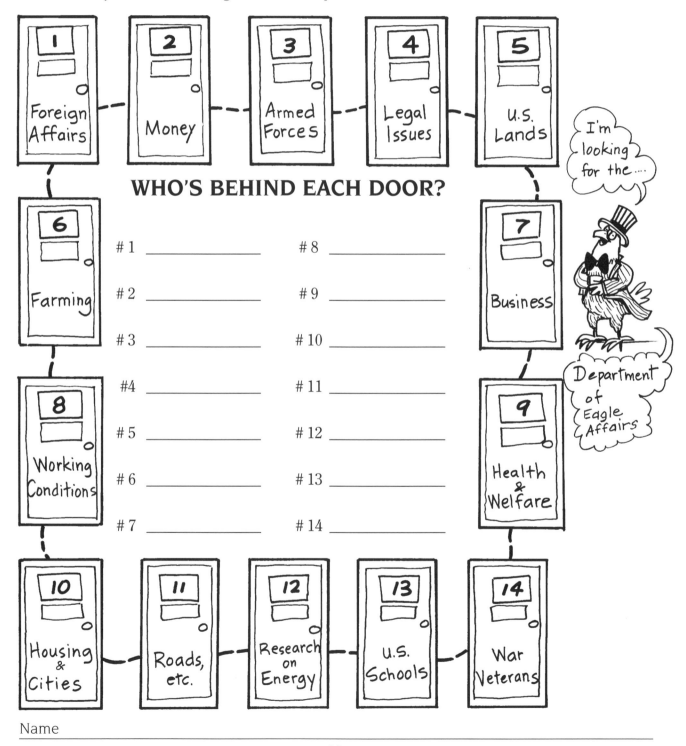

WHO'S BEHIND EACH DOOR?

1. Foreign Affairs
2. Money
3. Armed Forces
4. Legal Issues
5. U.S. Lands
6. Farming
7. Business
8. Working Conditions
9. Health & Welfare
10. Housing & Cities
11. Roads, etc.
12. Research on Energy
13. U.S. Schools
14. War Veterans

I'm looking for the.....

Department of Eagle Affairs

1 _____

2 _____

3 _____

#4 _____

5 _____

6 _____

7 _____

8 _____

9 _____

10 _____

11 _____

12 _____

13 _____

14 _____

Name _____

ACQUIRED AMERICAN ACRONYMS

There are more than two hundred different agencies and corporations that make up the Executive Branch of our government. Did you know that? They administer government programs in a wide variety of all areas of American life. We know many of these by their acronyms, (a word formed from the first letters or syllables of other words). Polish up your familiarity with their names and purposes.

Name as many of these as you can. Then write a brief description of what the agency or corporation does. See if you can earn 200 points or more.

1. **NASA** _____ (5pts)

(Description) _____ (10pts)

2. **IRS** _____ (5pts)

(Description) _____ (10pts)

3. **VA** _____ (5pts)

(Description) _____ (10pts)

4. **FBI** _____ (5pts)

(Description) _____ (10pts)

5. **CIA** _____ (5pts)

(Description) _____ (10pts)

6. **FHA** _____ (5pts)

(Description) _____ (10pts)

7. **OSHA** _____ (5pts)

(Description) _____ (10pts)

8. **INS** _____ (5pts)

(Description) _____ (10pts)

9. **BIA** _____ (5pts)

(Description) _____ (10pts)

10. **BLM** _____ (5pts)

(Description) _____ (10pts)

11. **NPS** _____ (5pts)

(Description) _____ (10pts)

12. **DEQ** _____ (5pts)

(Description) _____ (10pts)

13. **NOAA** _____ (5pts)

(Description) _____ (10pts)

14. **FDA** _____ (5pts)

(Description) _____ (10pts)

15. **FCC** _____ (5pts)

(Description) _____ (10pts)

16. **FAA** _____ (5pts)

(Description) _____ (10pts)

17. **FDIC** _____ (5pts)

(Description) _____ (10pts)

18. **FTC** _____ (5pts)

(Description) _____ (10pts)

How did you do?

Total points_____

Name _____

THE GRAND DESIGN OF CONGRESS

Make some sense of the maze of Congress while you brush up on your facts about the two houses of Congress.

Color the SENATE boxes red. Color the HOUSE OF REPRESENTATIVES boxes blue.
Draw a red path connecting facts about the SENATE.
Draw a blue path connecting facts about the HOUSE OF REPRESENTATIVES.

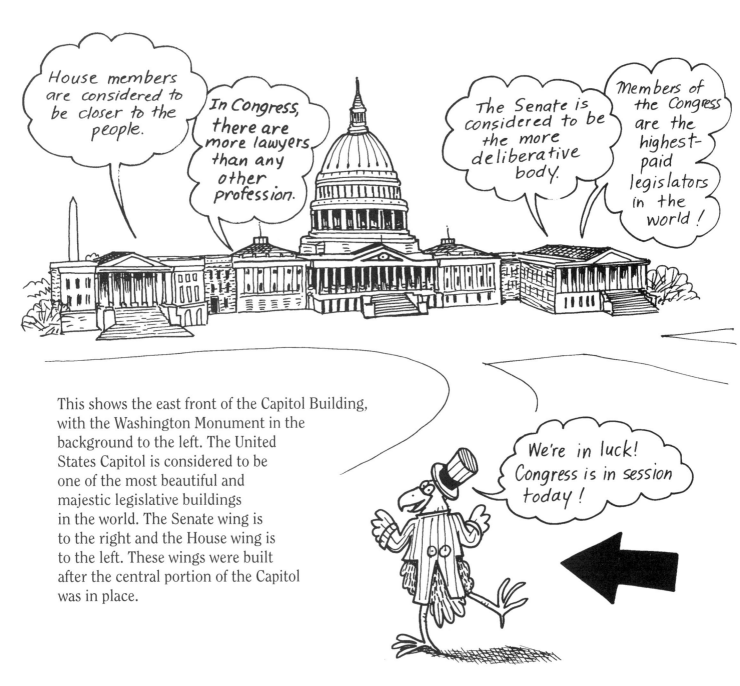

This shows the east front of the Capitol Building, with the Washington Monument in the background to the left. The United States Capitol is considered to be one of the most beautiful and majestic legislative buildings in the world. The Senate wing is to the right and the House wing is to the left. These wings were built after the central portion of the Capitol was in place.

Use with page 25.

Name

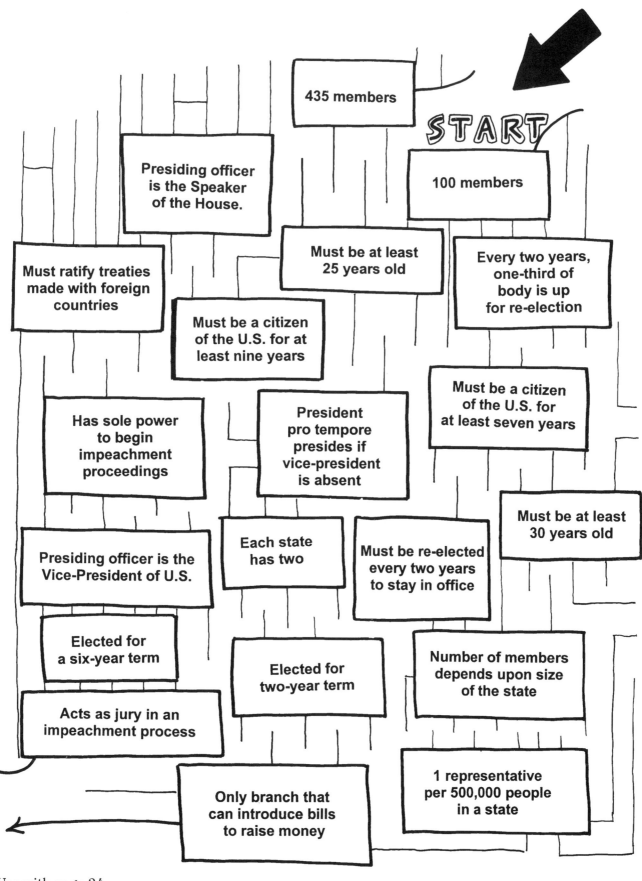

435 members

START

100 members

Presiding officer is the Speaker of the House.

Must be at least 25 years old

Every two years, one-third of body is up for re-election

Must ratify treaties made with foreign countries

Must be a citizen of the U.S. for at least nine years

Has sole power to begin impeachment proceedings

President pro tempore presides if vice-president is absent

Must be a citizen of the U.S. for at least seven years

Must be at least 30 years old

Presiding officer is the Vice-President of U.S.

Each state has two

Must be re-elected every two years to stay in office

Elected for a six-year term

Elected for two-year term

Number of members depends upon size of the state

Acts as jury in an impeachment process

Only branch that can introduce bills to raise money

1 representative per 500,000 people in a state

Use with page 24.

Name

UNDER THE DOME

Before you visit that building with the big dome, make sure you are all caught up on your facts about what goes on inside.

Use the words in the capitol dome to complete the statements about the workings of the Legislative Branch (Congress), as defined by the Constitution.

Words in the dome: quorum, expel, representative, Senate, privileges, majority, Congressional Record, recess, Capitol, two, Congress, laws, U.S. Government, House of Representatives, minority, rules, odd-numbered, meet, four, terms, adjourn, even-numbered

1. The American system of government is based on a _____ form of government.

2. Laws are passed by a _____ vote, which means one over half.

3. The smaller group of voting representatives is known as the _____ .

4. The Legislative Branch of our Federal government is called _____ .

5. Congress starts its meetings on the third day of January every _____ year.

6. The House of Representatives and the Senate meet in different chambers on opposite sides of the _____ in Washington, D.C.

7. Congress makes its own _____ governing its meetings.

8. Congress may _____ , or remove, one of its members for breaking its rules by a 2/3rds vote.

9. The record of all meetings of Congress is called the _____ .

10. Two _____ that members share are: they cannot be arrested when going to or from Congress, or while attending a session, and they cannot be sued or punished for anything they say in Congress.

11. There must be a _____ in order for a congressional meeting to be held. This means one person over half of the number of its members.

12. Neither the House nor the Senate may _____ without the consent of the other.

13. The _____ pays Congresspersons' salaries, and amounts are set by law.

14. Congressional meetings are called _____ , and last _____ years, with a _____ during the summer.

15. The major job of the Legislative branch of our government is to make _____ .

Name _____

WHAT CONGRESS CAN & CANNOT DO

Congress is not allowed to do everything! The *Constitution* grants many important powers to the Congress such as the power to coin money, declare war, and provide a military. The *Constitution* also says some things the Congress CANNOT do. Do you know the difference?

Egbert Eagle has to take a skill-sharpening test every six months. You take it, too. Tell which statements are true (T) and which ones are false (F). Correct any false statements by replacing the un-true part with the correct words.

_____ 1. The written powers specifically given to Congress by the *Constitution,* such as the power to declare war, are called enumerated powers.

_____ 2. Implied Powers are general powers that are stated in the *Constitution,* but are not clearly outlined.

_____ 3. Inherent powers are unlisted powers that Congress must have simply because it is a government and needs to run its affairs smoothly.

_____ 4. The "Elastic Clause" snaps the Congress back into its given limits if it abuses its power.

_____ 5. The Congress cannot take away a dead citizen's right of *Habeas Corpus*, except in cases of rebellion or invasion.

_____ 6. A "bill of attainder" is a law passed by the government that convicts and punishes a person without a trial.

_____ 7. *Ex post facto* means a crime against the U.S. Postal Service.

_____ 8. Two powers that individual states possess are the power to make treaties and the power to coin money.

_____ 9. Two powers of Congress are the power to tax products from an individual state and the power to issue titles of nobility.

_____ 10. Delegated powers are those given to the federal government.

_____ 11. The state and federal governments share concurrent powers.

_____ 12. State and Federal governments share reserved powers.

Name _____

27

BILLS ON THE MOVE

I asked my Congressman to propose a bill to create a new holiday— National Eagle Day!

What happens next?

Once a bill is written, you have to keep your eye on it— because it starts to MOVE. Sometimes a bill moves quickly, other times it moves slowly. But you always have to be on your toes, if you're going to follow it all the way until it becomes a law.

Just how does a bill become a law? There is a definite pattern to this. Read the description of the steps (A–M). They are out of order. Number the descriptions 1–13 to match the footsteps and show the path a bill takes on its way to becoming a law.

A
It then becomes law without the president's signature.

B
If the committee has approved a bill, it goes to the full House of Representatives or Senate to be debated and voted on.

C
The committee votes on the bill.

D
The president signs the bill into law.

E
The bill is introduced in both houses of Congress.

F
A member of Congress proposes a law. This proposal is called a bill. The person who proposes it is the *sponsor*.

Use with page 29.

Name

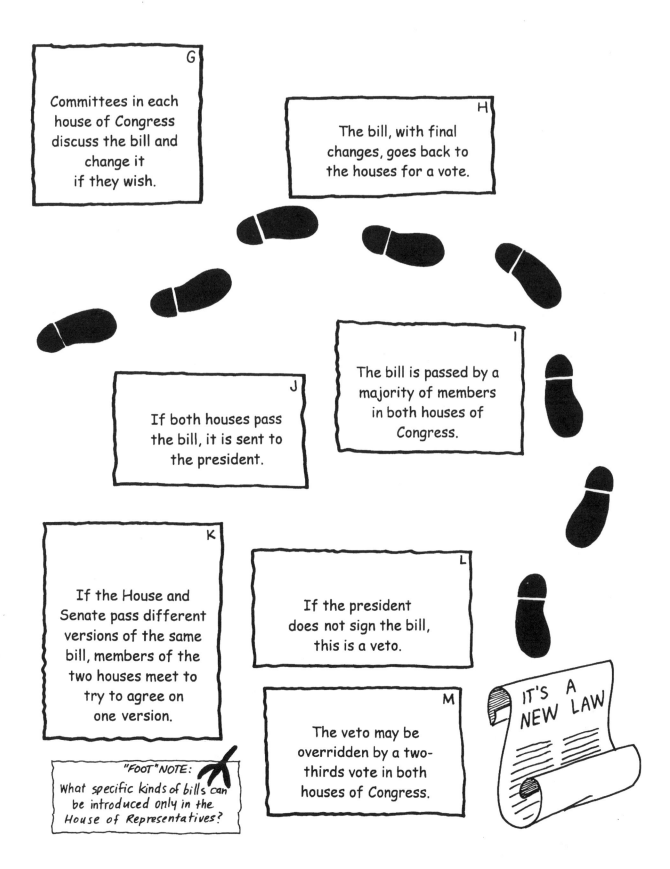

G Committees in each house of Congress discuss the bill and change it if they wish.

H The bill, with final changes, goes back to the houses for a vote.

I The bill is passed by a majority of members in both houses of Congress.

J If both houses pass the bill, it is sent to the president.

K If the House and Senate pass different versions of the same bill, members of the two houses meet to try to agree on one version.

L If the president does not sign the bill, this is a veto.

M The veto may be overridden by a two-thirds vote in both houses of Congress.

"FOOT"NOTE: What specific kinds of bills can be introduced only in the House of Representatives?

IT'S A NEW LAW

Use with page 28.

Name

SUPREME ORDER IN THE COURT

In the federal government, there are a bunch of officials who wear black robes a lot. These are members of the court system. The Supreme Court is the highest court in the country. Along with the lower courts, the nine Supreme Court justices (judges) are part of the branch of the U.S. government that interprets and explains the law.

This information about the judicial branch is in major disorder. The facts are all wrong. Find the error in every statement, and replace any words necessary to get the fact right.

SUPREME COURT

I belong to a select group of nine justices.

1. The first major body of the Judicial Branch is the Appeals Court.

2. Court justices need no previous legal knowledge and expertise.

3. The Supreme Court has no power to define the powers of Congress.

4. Supreme Court justices are appointed by the vice-president and approved by the Senate.

5. As of yet, there are no women serving on the Supreme Court.

6. The Judicial Branch passes laws.

7. A Supreme Court Justice serves for 12 years.

8. The Constitution did not describe the duties of the Supreme Court.

9. It is the courts' job to enforce laws.

10. The Constitution left it up to the President to determine the number of lower courts in the system.

11. The Court is never allowed to interpret the Constitution.

12. The Supreme Court Building is found in New York City.

13. There are 13 Supreme Court Justices.

14. There are two kinds of lower federal courts: county and appellate courts.

15. The appellate court is different from an appeals court.

16. Once appointed, a Supreme Court justice cannot be removed.

17. Federal Courts have the responsibility to hear all cases involving the laws and treaties of the U.S., but not those involving two or more states.

18. Four or more justices must agree before an opinion becomes the Supreme Court's official decision.

19. The courts of the judicial system only include federal courts.

20. By law, most people who lose a case in court have no right to appeal to a higher court.

Name _____

FAMOUS COURT DECISIONS

How does a court case get its name, anyway? Egbert tells the straight story about naming a case.

Some of the Supreme Court cases and court decisions stand out in history because of their impact on our society. Match the titles of these better-known cases with the resulting court decisions.

> The Supreme Court cases get their titles by using the names of the two sides involved. The first name is the one who lost a case in the lower court and is trying to appeal to the Supreme Court. The second name is the winner of the lower court who is now defending the lower court ruling.

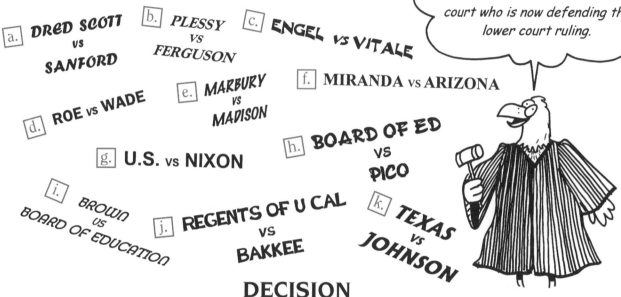

DECISION

_____ 1. Ruled that anyone arrested must be read a statement of their rights before being questioned or their statements cannot be used as evidence against them in court.

_____ 2. Ruled that executive privilege has its limits! The President had to turn over tapes as evidence in the Watergate investigation.

_____ 3. Ruled school segregation unconstitutional (overturning an earlier decision).

_____ 4. Ruled that the government can't stop a person from a dissenting view or action (in this case, flag-burning) because it finds it offensive.

_____ 5. The famous separate but equal (for blacks & whites) ruling of 1896.

_____ 6. Ruling declares that the Supreme Court can overrule a law of Congress.

_____ 7. Ruled that schools cannot require students to say prayers at school.

_____ 8. In 1868, the Supreme Court overruled the 14th Amendment and declared a slave was not a citizen and had no right to sue.

_____ 9. Ruled that states could no longer ban abortions.

_____ 10. Ruled that a school board can't ban books from a school library just because someone doesn't agree with the ideas in them.

_____ 11. A landmark ruling regarding affirmative action; the ruling left many questions and confusions about affirmative action.

Name

A POWER PUZZLER

Who's got the power in the United States government? That's a question that has several answers. When the Constitution was written, no one wanted the central government to swallow up the states. They wanted the states to remain strong and healthy. Federalism is the term used for sharing of power by the national and state governments.

Use puzzle pieces to show which powers are which.

Use RED for puzzle pieces that show reserved powers.
Use BLUE for delegated powers.
Use GREEN for concurrent powers.

Delegated powers *are given to the national government.*
Reserved powers *are held by the states.*
Concurrent powers *are shared by both.*

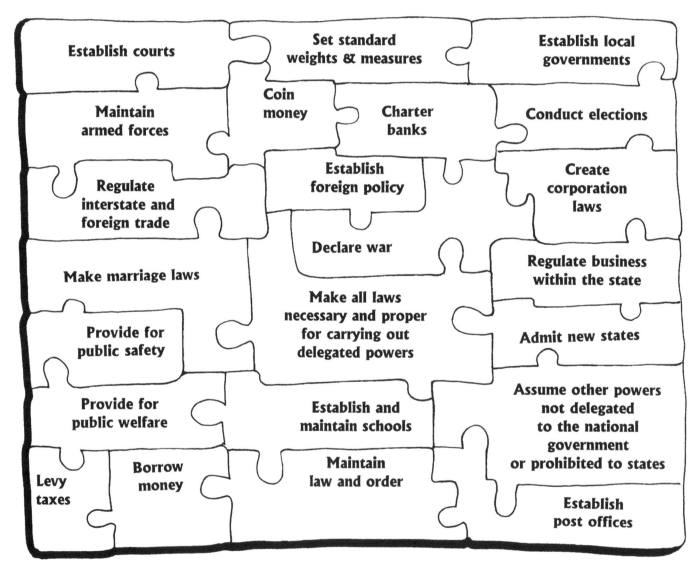

Establish courts

Set standard weights & measures

Establish local governments

Maintain armed forces

Coin money

Charter banks

Conduct elections

Regulate interstate and foreign trade

Establish foreign policy

Create corporation laws

Make marriage laws

Declare war

Regulate business within the state

Provide for public safety

Make all laws necessary and proper for carrying out delegated powers

Admit new states

Provide for public welfare

Establish and maintain schools

Assume other powers not delegated to the national government or prohibited to states

Levy taxes

Borrow money

Maintain law and order

Establish post offices

Name _____

ELECTION QUESTIONS & ANSWERS

There's nothing quite like an American election! Bands . . . balloons . . . banners . . . confetti . . . shouting . . . cheering . . . speeches . . . campaign buttons . . . and hours of television discussion. An election is a democratic process by which citizens select the people they want to represent them to run their government. But there is plenty of noise, excitement, and competition that goes along with that process!

Each ANSWER below has to do with something unique about the American election process. Write a QUESTION to match each answer. Set a time limit, and try to get over 100 points (10 points each). Don't forget to write a question.

1.
Question_____

_____
Answer: *the 15ᵗʰ Amendment*

2.
Question_____

_____
Answer: *the 26ᵗʰ Amendment*

3.
Question_____

_____
Answer: *the 1965 Voting Rights Act*

4.
Question_____

_____
Answer: *the "Motor-Voter" Bill*

5.
Question_____

_____
Answer: *the 19ᵗʰ amendment*

6.
Question_____

_____
Answer: *literacy tests & poll taxes*

7.
Question_____

_____
Answer: *the electoral vote*

8.
Question_____

_____
Answer: *representative democracy*

9.
Question_____

_____
Answer: *a primary election*

10.
Question_____

_____
Answer: *a campaign*

11.
Question_____

_____
Answer: *Republicans & Democrats*

12.
Question_____

_____
Answer: *Elizabeth Cady Stanton, Carrie Chapman, & Lucretia Mott*

Name

A VOTER'S VOCABULARY

If you are an American citizen, when you reach the age of 18, you will become eligible to use your right to vote. Since this is one of the most important rights in a democracy, why not begin getting ready for it now?

The word search on this page contains some voting vocabulary words you will need to understand to be an informed, intelligent voter. Read the clues on the next page. Fill each blank with the correct word, then circle the word in the puzzle. Words may be written up, down, forwards, backwards, or diagonally.

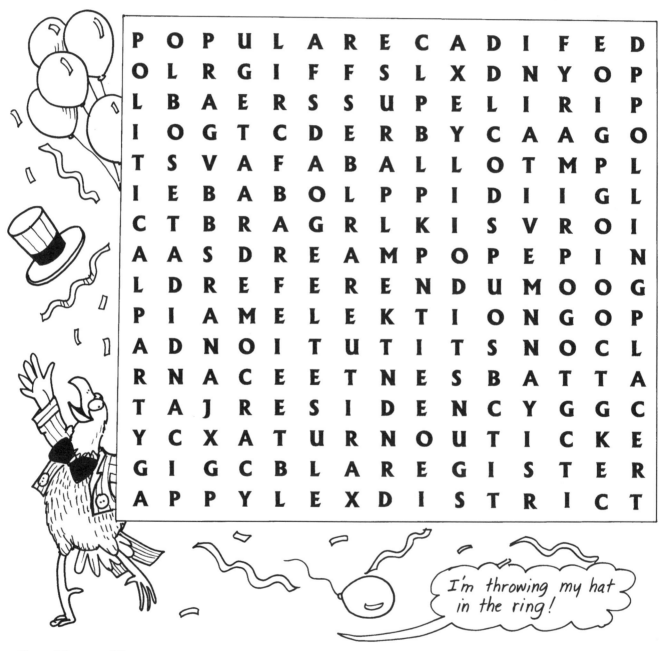

Use with page 35.

Name

A VOTER'S VOCABULARY

Read the clues below. Fill each blank with the correct word, then circle the word in the puzzle on page 34. Words may be written up, down, forwards, backwards, or diagonally.

1. A _____ requirement is a length of time someone must live in a state before being able to vote there.

2. A government that is governed by its people, who have the same basic rights and freedoms, is called a _____ .

3. The _____ is the document that assures and protects our rights, including the right to vote.

4. Voting to decide who will be our public officials is called an _____ .

5. People who are running for political offices are called _____ .

6. The list that a voter actually votes on is called a _____ .

7. A _____ is a statement that political parties set up of policies and principles for voters to consider.

8. An organization that puts forward candidates for political offices is called a _____ .

9. The _____ vote is the votes cast by individual voters in the presidential election.

10. A _____ election is held to choose candidates for the main election.

11. A _____ is a vote on a specific issue, like a city's budget or a building project.

12. A _____ is where people go to vote in their district.

13. To officially sign up to vote is to _____ .

14. A _____ is the number of eligible voters who actually vote in an election.

15. The place you live and are registered to vote is called your voting _____ .

16. _____ ballots are votes mailed in earlier by people who could not be present on an election day.

Use with page 34.

Name _____

THE PRESIDENTIAL LINK

Extra! Extra! Read All About It! Great, historical events took place in the growth of the U.S government and Economy. The news headlines tell the stories! What Presidents were in office when these events took place?

Read each of the headlines on this page and the next page. Link the American president in office at the time to each event. Write the correct name under each headline.

U.S. Presidents

George Washington
John Adams
Thomas Jefferson
James Madison
James Monroe
John Quincy Adams
Andrew Jackson
Martin Van Buren
William Henry Harrison
John Tyler
James K. Polk
Zachary Taylor
Millard Fillmore
Franklin Pierce
James Buchanan
Abraham Lincoln
Andrew Johnson
Ulysses S. Grant
Rutherford B. Hayes
James A. Garfield
Chester A. Arthur
Grover Cleveland
Benjamin Harrison
Grover Cleveland
William McKinley
Theodore Roosevelt
William Howard Taft
Woodrow Wilson
Warren G. Harding
Calvin Coolidge
Herbert Hoover
Franklin D. Roosevelt
Harry S. Truman
Dwight D. Eisenhower
John F. Kennedy
Lyndon B. Johnson
Richard M. Nixon
Gerald R. Ford
Jimmy Carter
Ronald Reagan
George Bush
William J. Clinton

1. 1993 Page News
Food Aid Sent To Starving Somali Millions

2. 1797 Gazette
XYZ Affair Causes Sensation!

3. 1929 Inquirer
Stock Market Crash!

4. 1825 News
ERIE CANAL COMPLETED

5. 1933 Herald
President Calls For NEW DEAL

6. 1848 Variety
Gold Found At Sutter's Mill

7. 1969 Times
CIVIL RIGHTS LEADER SLAIN

8. 1850 Post
Abolitionist Douglas To Speak

9. 1979 Star
SALT II Signing

Use with page 37.

Name

10 *1866 Mail*
13th Amendment Abolishes Slavery

11 *1981 Press*
Iran Hostages Freed As President Sworn In

12 **1900 Globe**
Waves of European Immigrants Flood U.S. Shores

13 *1912 Register*
Titanic Sinks!

14 *1791 Tribune*
President Inaugurated at Federal Hall

15 *1920 Monitor*
Women Win Right To Vote!

16 **1804 Times**
Lewis & Clark Begin Expedition

17 *1829 Tidings*
First "Westerner" Elected President

18 *1945 Ledger*
BOMB DROPPED ON HIROSHIMA

19 *1953 Chronicle*
BERLIN WALL GOES UP

20 *1962 Democrat*
Soviet Missiles In Cuba!

21 *1969 Dispatch*
MAN WALKS ON MOON

22 *1970 Times*
250,000 Protest Vietnam War

23 *1908 Free Press*
FORD INVENTS THE MODEL T

24 *1861 Daily*
States Form Confederacy

25 *1989 Sun-Times*
EXXON VALDEX SPILLS TONS

History on the Front Pages!

Use with page 36.

Name

PONDERING PATRIOTISM

You might be thrilled by fireworks on July 4th, love getting out of school on Veteran's Day, or be able to recognize an American bald eagle. But how often do you stop to ponder what the symbols and traditions of your country mean?

These are just of few of the words, ideas, symbols, or icons that represent national characteristics or values. Describe each one's meaning in your own words, as if you were explaining them to someone from outside the United States who knows nothing about them at all. Use the spaces below and on page 39.

1.

2.

3. *Thanksgiving*

4.

5.

6. *4th of JULY*

Use with page 39.

Name

1.

2. *abolition*

3. **FREEDOM**

4.

5.

6. **democracy**

Use with page 38.

Name

FAMOUS SPACES & PLACES

Your tour guide wants to take you on an adventure around the whole USA. Maybe you have been to some of these places already. If you have, keep a count of the ones you've visited. All of the spots on the tour are fascinating landmarks that tell the story of the people and places that make our country.

A. Write the number in RED of each event (see on page 41) on the spot on the map where it is located or happened.

B. Then put a RED STAR on your top five choices for visiting.

C. Circle in YELLOW those landmarks you have been to.

1. Both the Constitution and the Declaration of Independence were written in this town.

2. This state has the first planned city in the U.S., and is the birthplace of Martin Luther King Jr.

3. George Washington's home is in this state.

4. Visit the Empire State Building and the Statue of Liberty here!

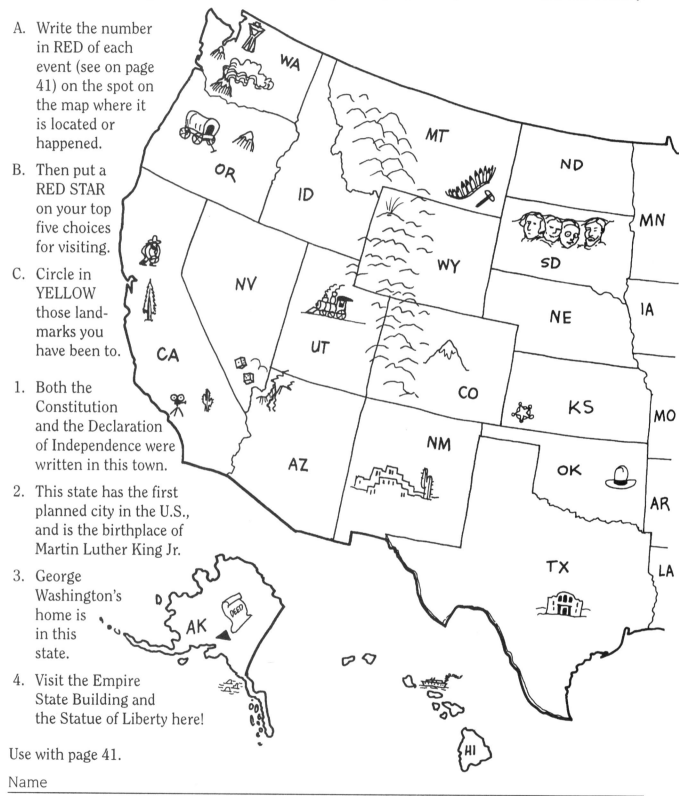

Use with page 41.

Name

5. The Grand Tetons and most of Yellowstone National Park are both found in this state.

6. The Revolutionary war battle at Valley Forge, and the Civil War battle at Gettysburg were fought in this state.

7. See Mt. Rushmore, the Crazy Horse and Wounded Knee Monuments, and the Badlands here!

8. Feast your eyes and take a hike in the Grand Canyon and the Painted Desert.

9. You'll see Lincoln's boyhood cabin and the Sears Tower here.

10. "Remember the Alamo" and the Rio Grande River are in this state!

11. The splendid Glacier Bay National Park and Denali Mountain Peak are found here.

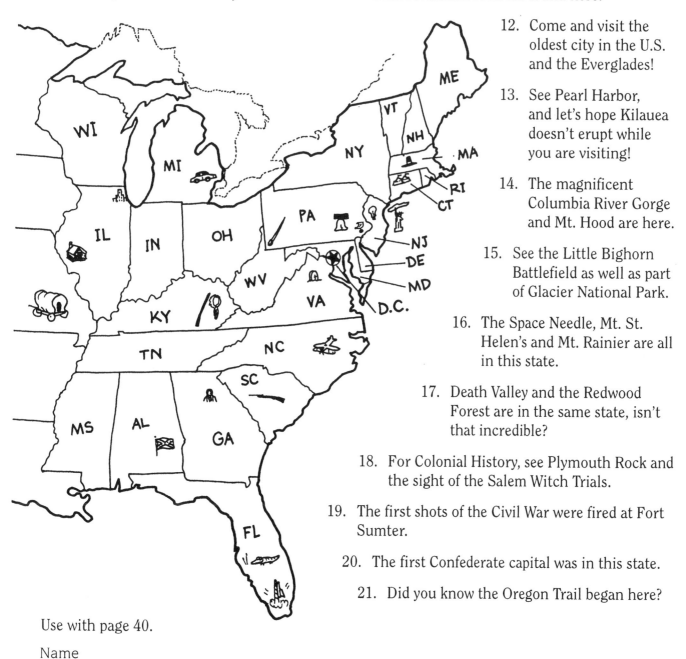

12. Come and visit the oldest city in the U.S. and the Everglades!

13. See Pearl Harbor, and let's hope Kilauea doesn't erupt while you are visiting!

14. The magnificent Columbia River Gorge and Mt. Hood are here.

15. See the Little Bighorn Battlefield as well as part of Glacier National Park.

16. The Space Needle, Mt. St. Helen's and Mt. Rainier are all in this state.

17. Death Valley and the Redwood Forest are in the same state, isn't that incredible?

18. For Colonial History, see Plymouth Rock and the sight of the Salem Witch Trials.

19. The first shots of the Civil War were fired at Fort Sumter.

20. The first Confederate capital was in this state.

21. Did you know the Oregon Trail began here?

Use with page 40.

Name

DO YOU KNOW YOUR REPRESENTATIVES?

Do you know who represents you? Have you ever written, phoned, faxed, or e-mailed any of them? You can! You can even communicate with the White House. The government representatives constantly keep in touch with the way people feel about issues. It helps when their constituents write them letters, phone them, e-mail, or fax them! Get online, use an almanac, or call your public library and find the names and any addresses, phone numbers, fax numbers, or e-mails for your representatives!

I'm going to hang this on my bulletin board!

FEDERAL GOVERNMENT

THE WHITE HOUSE

Your representative: President _____

Address: _____

Phone: _____

Fax or e-mail: _____

U.S. CONGRESS: YOUR SENATORS

1. Senator _____

Address: _____

Phone: _____

Fax or e-mail: _____

2. Senator _____

Address: _____

Phone: _____

Fax or e-mail: _____

YOUR REPRESENTATIVE IN THE HOUSE

Representative: _____

Address: _____

Phone: _____

Fax or e-mail: _____

STATE GOVERNMENT

GOVERNOR _____

Address: _____

Phone: _____

Fax or e-mail: _____

STATE SENATOR _____

Address: _____

Phone: _____

Fax or e-mail: _____

STATE HOUSE REPRESENTATIVE

_____

Address: _____

Phone: _____

Fax or e-mail: _____

LOCAL GOVERNMENT

MAYOR OF YOUR TOWN OR CITY

_____

Address: _____

Phone, Fax or e-mail: _____

COUNTY COMMISSIONER

_____

Address: _____

Phone, Fax or e-mail: _____

CITY COUNCIL REPRESENTATIVE

_____

Address: _____

Phone, Fax or e-mail: _____

SOMEONE ON A LOCAL BOARD

(such as a parks commission or school board)

_____

Address: _____

Phone, Fax or e-mail: _____

Name _____

YOU HOLD THE KEY

It's really true! You do hold the key to representative democracy in YOUR hands. YOU, THE CITIZEN must PARTICIPATE in order for democracy to work. Now that you've gathered all those addresses for your local, state and national representatives . . . put them to work for you! Pay attention to issues around you, and let your leaders in your representative democracy hear from you.

Here are some ideas about good citizenship to get you started:

Remember! Participation is the key to Representative Democracy !!

1. It's important to be informed about political issues, both in Washington and right in your own backyard. Name TWO issues that concern you, or that may affect you and your family or community, or the world. Include one that is national or global in scope, and one that is "right in your own backyard." List them here:

2. Read newspapers, news magazines, watch the TV news programs, listen to the radio news, look on the Internet. Name some of your favorite ways that keep you informed on the issues that you named in #1. List them here.

3. Volunteering for political campaigns or community service are also ways to help out and be a good citizen. Name some organizations and volunteer programs that you think are deserving of people's help and attention. List them here:

4. Even if you are too young to vote, you can think about how you WOULD vote on an issue of for an candidate. Write down one person or initiative that you would say YES to, and one you would say NO to.
Tell why.

5. Get involved when you become an adult, and Run for Office! It could be President, but it could mean serving on local boards, park commissions, city councils, etc. Name FIVE local boards or organizations that people in your community give time and effort to that make where you live a better place:

Name _____

SHINING STAR CITIZENS

How did these people earn a star? Find out why these women citizens might be called "shining star citizens." What have they contributed to our society?

Match their accomplishments or contributions to society with their names. Write the number from the description on page 45 onto the right star.

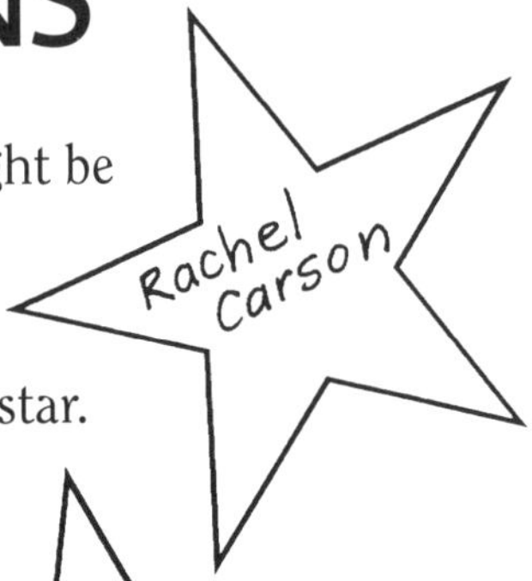

Rachel Carson

Sandra Day O'Connor

Jane Addams

Janet Reno

Rosa Parks

Betty Friedan

Harriet Tubman

Geraldine Ferraro

Liliuokalani

Eleanor Roosevelt

Coretta Scott King

Sojourner Truth

Mary Mcleod Bethune

Mother Jones

Sacajawea

Sarah Winnemucca

.....and my mother, Betsy Ross Eagle!

Use with page 45.

Name _____

1. "Conductor" on the Underground Railroad; helped 200–300 slaves make their way to freedom.

2. Forceful speaker against slavery and for women's rights who was once a slave herself.

3. Native American humanitarian who guided Lewis and Clark's Corps of Discovery through the West.

4. Daughter of a Paiute Chief who was an activist and spokesperson for Indian rights.

5. Politician who was the first woman to run for Vice-president.

6. Activist and Union organizer who helped workers gain better pay and working conditions.

7. Refused to yield her seat to a white person on a segregated bus in Montgomery, Alabama and became a major catalyst to the Civil Rights Movement.

8. Born the 15th child of a slave, this woman was later in charge of Minority Affairs in the National Youth Administration, and became vice-president of both the NAACP & the Urban League.

9. First woman Attorney General, under President Clinton.

10. First female appointed to the Supreme Court.

11. The only American native born queen, spokesperson, and activist for the Hawaiian native peoples.

12. Author of *The Feminine Mystique*, helped found the National Organization of Women.

13. After her husband, Martin Luther King, Jr., died, she became a prominent voice in the Civil Rights Movement.

14. First lady activist, spokesperson, "the eyes of the president," who worked to improve the lot of the poor and disenfranchised of America.

15. Persuasive author who wrote *Silent Spring*, about the dangers to the environment.

16. Nobel Peace Prize recipient and founder of Hull House, a settlement for the poor.

What citizens in YOUR community or neighborhood deserve a star for contributing something to society? Write the name of three people you would label as shining star citizens.

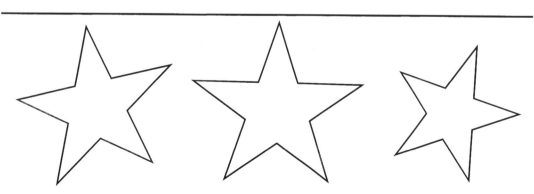

Use with page 44.

Name _____

THE HEAD FED

I keep my money in a safe place.

PENNY BANK

Can you imagine how much money it takes to run the United States Government? The Federal Reserve Board probably has a good idea about the country's finances. The Federal Reserve, fondly known as "The Fed," is the main bank of the government's banking system.

Show your knowledge about the "The Fed" and the U.S. economic system. Find the missing word in each statement about the Federal Reserve.

bank	Boston	controls	credit cards	money	sells
Washington D.C.	supervises	paper	checking	checks	phone calls
New York City	credit	coins	buys	diamonds	twelve

1. The Federal Reserve is the government's _____ .

2. The Reserve is divided into _____ regional banks across the country.

3. Its main headquarters is in _____ .

4. A List of the "The Fed's Functions are:

A. _____ the amount of money in circulation.

B. Regulates and _____ banks and banking practices.

C. Manages laws that protect consumers who want _____ .

D. Makes sure that there is enough _____ and coin in circulation.

E. Takes care of the government's _____ accounts.

F. _____ and _____ dollars on foreign exchange markets.

G. Processes millions of _____ each day that pass between banks.

Name _____

SOME TAXING QUESTIONS

What do roads, armed forces, libraries, bridges, fire protection, and garbage collection have in common? The answer is TAXES. Citizens and businesses help pay for all of these things and services by paying taxes to city, state, and federal governments.

Match each tax word with its definition. Put the letter of the word next to the number of the definition.

_____ 1. Money governments collect from people and businesses.

_____ 2. A tax on the sale of goods and some services, usually added on to the price of the item.

_____ 3. An extra cost added on to the original cost of an item.

_____ 4. Companies pay taxes on the amount of this they make.

_____ 5. A tax that people pay on the money they make throughout the year.

_____ 6. Money received from employment.

_____ 7. Money received from investments like savings accounts, stocks, or bonds.

_____ 8. Excused from paying taxes.

_____ 9. A group, like a church or charitable organization that isn't formed for the purpose of profit (is tax-exempt).

_____ 10. A federal system of financial support for retired workers or those unable to work.

A. PROFIT

B. EARNED INCOME

C. NON-PROFIT

D. CURRENCY

E. SURCHARGE

F. SALES TAX

G. TAX RETURN

H. TAX-EXEMPT

I. TAXES

J. SOCIAL SECURITY

K. WELFARE

L. INCOME TAX

M. UNEARNED INCOME

Some of my taxes are going for an Eagle Preserve on Federal property!

Egbert Eagle
Skyline Eyrie
U.S.A.
Pay To: I.R.S.
Amount: $17.76
Amount: Seventeen dollars + 76/100
E.G. Eagle
for: taxes

Name _____

THE BIG PICTURE

What is THE BIG PICTURE of money in our world today? It's the ECONOMY! And what is the economy? It includes people, natural resources, and all the things people produce and consume. These "things" are called "Goods and Services" in common economic terms.

Solve the crossword puzzle below by "coming to terms" with the definitions and words of some important economic terms and principles you need to know in today's world of money. Use the clues on page 49.

I'm rushing to invest my "nest egg" in the market!

Use with page 49.

Name

ACROSS

1. Goods brought into one country from another are _____ .
3. During a _____ , businesses don't sell as much, there are fewer jobs, and people have less money to spend.
4. _____ is income paid by the government to people who need it to live.
6. _____ happens when more than one business sells the same product.
7. _____ is the chance of losing money.
8. If the expenses for producing an item are more than what you can sell it for, you will experience a _____ .
11. Money owed when you buy something on credit or borrow is _____ .
13. _____ is money a person pays to borrow money.
15. When you put money away to be used later, you are _____ .
17. Someone who starts and manages a business is called an _____ .
18. _____ is determined by how many consumers want to buy a product.
19. A Supreme Court judge and a national parks ranger work for the government in the _____ sector.
20. _____ is money loaned, usually for a fee, that must be paid back.
22. The money left over after all of a business's expenses are paid is called a _____ .
23. A _____ can happen when a recession goes on for a long time.

DOWN

1. _____ is an economic condition characterized by rising prices.
2. _____ is the amount of goods and services available to consumers.
5. When you spend your allowance and buy a new CD, you are being a _____ .
7. The raw materials, supplies, or money someone has to use for products or services are called _____
9. A risk of money to get something in return is called an _____ .
10. If you have no job, you are _____ .
12. A period of time when the amount of business increases is called _____ .
14. If a person is working for him or herself or for a company or business, he or she is in the _____ sector.
16. A worker who makes something people want to buy is called a _____ .
17. A business not required to pay taxes is called _____ .
21. The savings _____ is the percent of income that people save.

Use with page 48.

Name

DUBIOUS SPEECHES

Egbert is making some speeches about government and economy facts. He's a bit over-tired after a long day of guiding people on tours. Does he have all the facts straight or is he confused? Write TRUE or FALSE next to each of Egbert's proclamations.

1. Wall Street is a symbol of the U.S. financial world.

2. Justices on the Supreme Court serve a life term.

3. Inflation is an economic condition characterized by falling prices.

4. A member of Congress may not be arrested while attending a session of Congress.

5. The electoral college is a place where senators go to study.

6. The vice-president is the head of his or her political party.

7. The FAA is a group that oversees space exploration.

8. The Treasury Department is the central bank of the U.S.

9. Enumerated powers are powers clearly given to the Congress by the Constitution.

10. A senator is elected for a 6-year term.

11. A state can make a treaty with another country.

12. To be president, a person must have been born in the U.S.

13. The cabinet members are the president's closest advisors.

Name

APPENDIX

CONTENTS

UNITED STATES PRESIDENTS

	PRESIDENT	DATES IN OFFICE	PARTY	VICE PRESIDENT
1.	George Washington	1789-1797	None	John Adams
2.	John Adams	1797-1801	Federalist	Thomas Jefferson
3.	Thomas Jefferson	1801-1809	Republican	Aaron Burr; George Clinton
4.	James Madison	1809-1817	Republican	George Clinton; Elbridge Gerry
5.	James Monroe	1817-1825	Republican	Daniel D. Tompkins
6.	John Quincy Adams	1825-1829	Republican	John C. Calhoun
7.	Andrew Jackson	1829-1837	Democratic	John C. Calhoun; Martin Van Buren
8.	Martin Van Buren	1837-1841	Democratic	Richard M. Johnson
9.	William Henry Harrison	1841	Whig	John Tyler
10.	John Tyler	1841-1845	Whig	
11.	James K. Polk	1845-1849	Democratic	George M. Dallas
12.	Zachary Taylor	1849-1850	Whig	Millard Fillmore
13.	Millard Fillmore	1850-1853	Whig	
14.	Franklin Pierce	1853-1857	Democratic	William R. King
15.	James Buchanan	1857-1861	Democratic	John C. Breckenridge
16.	Abraham Lincoln	1861-1865	Republican	Hannibal Hamlin; Andrew Johnson
17.	Andrew Johnson	1865-1869	Republican	
18.	Ulysses S. Grant	1869-1877	Republican	Schuyler Colfax; Henry Wilson
19.	Rutherford B. Hayes	1877-1881	Republican	William A. Wheeler
20.	James A. Garfield	1881	Republican	Chester A. Arthur
21.	Chester A. Arthur	1881-1885	Republican	
22.	Grover Cleveland	1885-1889	Democratic	Thomas P. Hendricks
23.	Benjamin Harrison	1889-1893	Republican	Levi P. Morton
24.	Grover Cleveland	1893-1897	Democratic	Adlai E. Stevenson
25.	William McKinley	1897-1901	Republican	Garrett A. Hobart; Theodore Roosevelt
26.	Theodore Roosevelt	1901-1909	Republican	Charles W. Fairbanks
27.	William Howard Taft	1909-1913	Republican	James S. Sherman
28.	Woodrow Wilson	1913-1921	Democratic	Thomas R. Marshall
29.	Warren G. Harding	1921-1923	Republican	Calvin Coolidge
30.	Calvin Coolidge	1923-1929	Republican	Charles G. Dawes
31.	Herbert Hoover	1929-1933	Republican	Charles Curtis
32.	Franklin D. Roosevelt	1933-1945	Democratic	John Nance Garner, Henry Wallace, Harry S. Truman
33.	Harry S. Truman	1945-1953	Democratic	Alben W. Barkley
34.	Dwight D. Eisenhower	1953-1961	Republican	Richard M. Nixon
35.	John F. Kennedy	1961-1963	Democratic	Lyndon B. Johnson
36.	Lyndon B. Johnson	1963-1969	Democratic	Hubert H. Humphrey
37.	Richard M. Nixon	1969-1974	Republican	Spiro T. Agnew; Gerald R. Ford
38.	Gerald R. Ford	1974-1977	Republican	Nelson Rockefeller
39.	Jimmy Carter	1977-1981	Democratic	Walter F. Mondale
40.	Ronald Reagan	1981-1989	Republican	George H. Bush
41.	George Bush	1989-1993	Republican	J. Danforth Quayle
42.	William J. Clinton	1993-	Democratic	Albert Gore

Basic Skills/U.S. History 6-8+

U.S. CABINET DEPARTMENTS AND OFFICERS

DEPARTMENT	AREA OF OVERSIGHT	OFFICIAL
Department of State	foreign affairs	Secretary of State
Department of the Treasury	money	Secretary of the Treasury
Department of Defense	armed forces	Secretary of Defense
Department of Justice	legal issues	Attorney General
Department of the Interior	U.S. lands	Secretary of the Interior
Department of Agriculture	farming	Secretary of Agriculture
Department of Commerce	business	Secretary of Commerce
Department of Labor	working conditions	Secretary of Labor
Department of Health and Human Services	health & welfare	Secretary of Health and Human Services
Department of Housing and Urban Development	housing & cities	Secretary of Housing and Urban Development
Department of Transportation	roads	Secretary of Transportation
Department of Energy	energy research	Secretary of Energy
Department of Education	schools	Secretary of Education
Department of Veterans Affairs	war veterans	Secretary of Veterans Affairs

GOVERNMENT AGENCIES & CORPORATIONS
(SELECTED)

ATF: Bureau of Alcohol, Tobacco & Firearms

BIA: Bureau of Indian Affairs

BLM: Bureau of Land Management

CDCP: Centers for Disease Control & Prevention

CIA: Central Intelligence Agency

CPSC: Consumer Product Safety Commission

DEA: Drug Enforcement Agency

DEQ: Department of Environmental Quality

EPA: Environmental Protection Agency

FAA: Federal Aviation Administration

FBI: Federal Bureau of Investigation

FCC: Federal Communications Commission

FDA: Food & Drug Administration

FDIC: Federal Deposit Insurance Corporation

FEMA: Federal Emergency Management Agency

FHA: Federal Highway Administration

FTC: Federal Trade Commission

INS: Immigration & Naturalization Service

IRS: Internal Revenue Service

NASA: National Aeronautic Space Administration

NAEC: National Atomic Energy Commission

NEA: National Endowment for the Arts

NFWS: National Fish & Wildlife Service

NFS: National Forest Service

NIH: National Institutes of Health

NLRB: National Labor Relations Board

NPS: National Park Service

NTSB: National Transportation Safety Board

NOAA: National Oceanic & Atmospheric Administration

OSHA: Occupational Health & Safety Administration

SBA: Small Business Administration

SEC: Securities & Exchange Commission

USFS: U.S. Forest Service

USPS: U.S. Postal Service

VA: Veteran's Administration

GLOSSARY OF GOVERNMENT & ECONOMIC TERMS

absentee ballot: a vote mailed in before the election by people who cannot go to the polls on election day

amendment: a change or addition to a law

Articles of the Constitution: the seven sections that make up the main body of the Constitution

balance of power: equal military and economic strength between 2 or more nations

balanced budget: a budget in which the amount of money going out is equal to or less than the amount of money coming in

ballot initiative: an issue placed on a ballot by citizens to be voted upon in an election

bear market: a period in the stock market when the market is does poorly and stock prices fall

Bill of Rights: the first ten amendments to the U.S. Constitution

bill: a document which is presented to Congress as a proposal for a law

budget: a plan to show how a person, business, or organization will spend its money

bull market: a period in the stock market when the market does well and stock prices rise

business: an enterprise that sells goods or services for money

cabinet: officials who head government agencies and advise the president

candidate: a person who runs for a political office

capitalism: an economic system where individuals control production of goods, and government intervention is limited

checks and balances: the system in which the three branches of government have powers to limit the other branches so that no one branch becomes too powerful

competition: businesses selling the same product as another business

concurrent powers: powers that are to be shared by the national and state governments

Congress: the legislative branch of government made up of the Senate and House of Representatives

Constitution: the U.S. written plan of government

consumer: someone who buys and uses goods and services

credit: money loaned, usually for a fee

currency: any kind of money that is used for exchange in an economy

debt: the amount of money that has been borrowed or the amount of money owed when something is bought on credit

Declaration of Independence: the document adopted by the Second Continental Congress in 1776 that declared American independence from Great Britain and listed the reasons for this action

delegated powers: powers that are specifically given to the national government by the Constitution

demand: the level of desire that consumers have for a product or service

democracy: the form of government in which power is vested in the people and exercised by them through a system of free elections

depression: a period of steep decline in business activity, usually with high levels of unemployment

district: the place where someone lives and registers to vote

dividend: a share of the profits from a business paid to a stockholder

Dow Jones Industrial Average: a number that shows the average closing prices of a group of selected stocks

earned income: money received for doing a job

economy: the system of using resources and humans to produce and sell goods and services

election: an event where citizens vote to choose political leaders or to approve measures

electoral college: group of electors that elect the president and vice president of the U.S.

employee: a person who earns money by working for someone else

employer: a person or company that pays other people to work

entrepreneur: a person who develops a business

executive branch: the branch of the U.S. government responsible for enforcing laws

expansion: a period of time in which the amount of business in an area increases

exports: goods that are sent from one country to be sold in another

Federal Reserve: the main central bank of the United States

Great Depression: the economic crisis from 1929 to 1940

House of Representatives: one of two houses of Congress; states are represented by size of their population

impeachment: formal charge of wrongdoing brought against an elected official of the federal government

imports: goods that are purchased from another country

income: money a person gets from wages, investments, profits, or other sources

income tax: a tax paid to a government on someone's income

inflation: an economic condition characterized by rising prices

interest: the money paid for borrowing money or money paid for using someone else's money

investment: risking money to get something in return

judicial branch: the branch of the U.S. government responsible for interpreting laws

justice: a judge

legislative branch: the branch of the U.S. government responsible for making laws

loss: money that a business loses when the costs of producing products exceeds the earnings from selling them

mint: a place where coins are made; to make coin money

mortgage: a loan given to pay for a house, building or property

mutual fund: a company that sells stock in itself and uses the money to invest in other companies

national debt: the amount of money owed by the national government

need: something that a person or group of persons must have

New Deal: Franklin Roosevelt's program to revive the country from the Great Depression

nonprofit: a business that does not intend to make a profit

platform: a statement by a candidate or political party that is a set of principles or ideas they want to pursue if elected

president: the elected head of the executive branch of government

president pro tempore: the senator chosen by the Senate to be the presiding officer in the senate when the vice president is absent

political party: an organization that approves candidates for political offices and sets a platform of policies to promote

polling place: a place where people go to vote in their district

primary election: an election held to decide who the candidates will be on the ballots in the regular election

private sector: the part of the economy that is produced by businesses and individuals

producer: people or businesses that create or provide goods and/or services

profit: money a business makes after all its expenses are paid

public sector: the part of the economy that is produced by the government

ratify: to approve

recession: a period of time in the economy when the demand for goods declines and the flow of money decreases; usually accompanied by a period of rising unemployment

referendum: a vote on a specific issue, such as a city's budget or a building project

register: to officially sign up to vote

representative: an elected government official who serves in the House of Representatives

reserved powers: powers that only states have

residency: the requirement of a length of time someone must live in a state before being able to vote there or qualify for political office

revenue bills: laws which have to do with raising money for the government

salary: the money paid to a worker for a job done

sales tax: a tax that is added to the price of goods by the seller

savings: money that is put away to be used later

Senate: the house of Congress in which each state is represented by two senators

senator: an elected government representative who serves in the Senate

services: work done for other people

separation of powers: the concept of U.S. government that power is spread among branches of the federal government and between the federal and state governments

Social Security: a federal system that gives financial support from the federal government to retired workers and to others unable to work because of a disability

Speaker of the House: the presiding officer in the House of Representatives

stock: a part of ownership in a company that is sold to the public

stock market: the place where shares of stock for many different companies can be bought and sold

supply: the amount of a good or service that is available to consumers

Supreme Court: the highest U.S. court of appeals, composed of nine justices

taxes: money that a government collects from people and businesses

tax-exempt: an organization that is not required to pay taxes

treason: actions that attempt to overthrow the government

unearned income: money someone gets from sources other than working

unemployment: rate the total number of people out of work in an area

veto: the presidential power to reject bills passed by Congress

wages: money paid to an employee for a job

Wall Street: a street in New York City where much financial business is conducted; it has become the symbol for the financial world in the U.S.

want: something that someone would like to have but does not need

welfare: income that is paid to someone by the government because it is needed for them to live

55

U.S. GOVERNMENT, ECONOMY, & CITIZENSHIP SKILLS TEST

Match each news headline with the president who was in office at the time. Write the correct letter on the line.

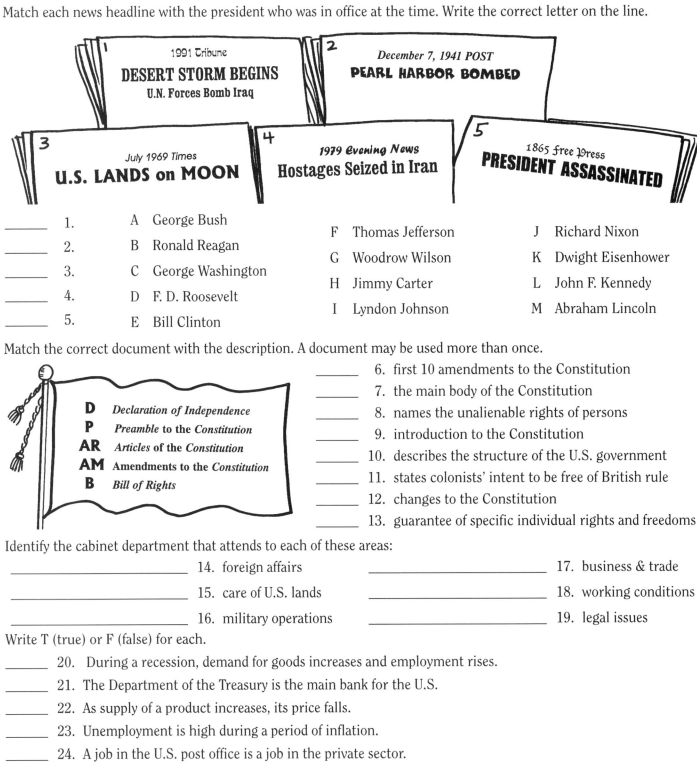

1991 Tribune
DESERT STORM BEGINS
U.N. Forces Bomb Iraq

December 7, 1941 POST
PEARL HARBOR BOMBED

July 1969 Times
U.S. LANDS on MOON

1979 Evening News
Hostages Seized in Iran

1865 Free Press
PRESIDENT ASSASSINATED

_____ 1.
_____ 2.
_____ 3.
_____ 4.
_____ 5.

A   George Bush
B   Ronald Reagan
C   George Washington
D   F. D. Roosevelt
E   Bill Clinton

F   Thomas Jefferson
G   Woodrow Wilson
H   Jimmy Carter
I   Lyndon Johnson

J   Richard Nixon
K   Dwight Eisenhower
L   John F. Kennedy
M   Abraham Lincoln

Match the correct document with the description. A document may be used more than once.

D   *Declaration of Independence*
P   *Preamble to the Constitution*
AR   *Articles of the Constitution*
AM   *Amendments to the Constitution*
B   *Bill of Rights*

_____ 6. first 10 amendments to the Constitution
_____ 7. the main body of the Constitution
_____ 8. names the unalienable rights of persons
_____ 9. introduction to the Constitution
_____ 10. describes the structure of the U.S. government
_____ 11. states colonists' intent to be free of British rule
_____ 12. changes to the Constitution
_____ 13. guarantee of specific individual rights and freedoms

Identify the cabinet department that attends to each of these areas:

_____ 14. foreign affairs
_____ 15. care of U.S. lands
_____ 16. military operations

_____ 17. business & trade
_____ 18. working conditions
_____ 19. legal issues

Write T (true) or F (false) for each.

_____ 20. During a recession, demand for goods increases and employment rises.

_____ 21. The Department of the Treasury is the main bank for the U.S.

_____ 22. As supply of a product increases, its price falls.

_____ 23. Unemployment is high during a period of inflation.

_____ 24. A job in the U.S. post office is a job in the private sector.

Name _____

Basic Skills/U.S. History 6-8+

Could these events be true? Write YES or NO for each one.

_____ 25. Elizabeth Gustavez serves as the U.S. president from 2004–2014.

_____ 26. 40-year old J. Van Plough, born in Sweden, a citizen of the U.S. for 5 years, is elected to the U.S. House of Representatives.

_____ 27. In the year 2005, T. Romano, the newly-elected Republican president of the U.S., becomes the chief of the Republican Party.

_____ 28. 24-year old Anna Maria Tomei, a U.S. citizen for 10 years, is elected to the U.S. House of Representatives.

_____ 29. An education bill with 75 YES votes in the Senate does not pass.

_____ 30. In 2008, the U.S. Senate convicts a Supreme Court justice of impeachable offenses.

_____ 31. In 2001, the president declares war on a European country.

_____ 32. Jay Turani, a 20-year U.S. resident born in Nigeria, becomes U.S. president.

_____ 33. In one session of Congress, the number of Representatives in the House outnumbers the number of Senators.

_____ 34. 30-year old Justine Tallis is not approved as a Supreme Court justice because she is too young.

_____ 35. A U.S. president, too ill to carry out his duties, is replaced by the president pro tempore of the Senate.

_____ 36. A health bill passes the Senate with only 26 Senators present to vote.

_____ 37. $\frac{2}{3}$ of the Senators vote to expel a Senator for breaking the Senate's rules.

_____ 38. While attending a meeting of the House of Representatives, a representative is arrested for a traffic violation.

_____ 39. On Monday, the president decides to give a raise to the Congress, effective the following Tuesday.

_____ 40. 130 Senators vote YES on a bill to save Social Security.

_____ 41. 40-year old Samuel Jones, a natural-born U.S. citizen living in California, is elected to serve in the U.S. Senate as a representative of Idaho.

_____ 42. Ten witnesses see Jane Public commit a terrible crime and she is convicted immediately, without a trial.

_____ 43. A new Supreme Court justice, appointed by the president, is quickly approved by the Senate.

_____ 44. On July 1, a law is passed against smoking. Tanya Seers is arrested on July 2 because she broke this law back on June 1.

Match the agency or corporation with its responsibility. Write the correct acronym.

_____ 45. radio & TV licensing

_____ 46. tax collection

_____ 47. immigration

_____ 48. emergency preparation

_____ 49. quality of the environment

_____ 50. international clue gathering

CIA   IRS   INS

FDIC FTC FCC

DEA   DEQ SEC

USPS NPS

FEMA

NASA EPA

Name _____

Basic Skills/U.S. History 6-8+

Match these voting terms with their meanings.

_____ 51. place where a resident lives and votes

_____ 52. election held to choose candidates for main election

_____ 53. votes of individual voters

_____ 54. issue placed on a ballot by voters

_____ 55. to sign up for voting

_____ 56. statement of principles of a political party

D. popular vote

E. absentee vote

F. electoral vote

G. referendum

A. political party   H. district

B. primary   I. platform

C. initiative   J. register

Write a letter (see codes) to show which governmental branch or official has each of these powers.

P = President

C = Congress

H = House of Representatives

S = Senate

SC = Supreme Court

_____ 57. coins money

_____ 58. levies taxes

_____ 59. can impeach an official

_____ 60. can over-ride a veto

_____ 61. can declare a law unconstitutional

_____ 62. appoints justices to the Supreme Court

_____ 63. serves as jury in an impeachment trial

_____ 64. makes treaties

_____ 65. approves appointments

_____ 66. can veto a law

Write the correct economic term to match each meaning.

67. money left over after expenses are paid _____

68. money risked to gain something _____

69. income gained from doing a job _____

70. the desire consumers have for a product _____

71. fee paid for borrowing money _____

72. an extra charge added to the cost of an item _____

73. two businesses selling the same service or product _____

74. tax paid on the money someone makes _____

supply   profit

demand   profit

sales tax   nonprofit

interest   loss

income tax   credit

unearned   competition

surcharge   debt

surcharge   investment

earned

Write the answer on the line.

75. Who is the leader of the Senate? _____

76. What position is held by the leader of the House of Representatives? _____

77. Where does the Congress meet? _____

78. What is the number of Supreme Court Justices? _____

79. Who is the Chief of the U.S. Armed Forces? _____

80. Name the three unalienable rights named in the Declaration of Independence.

_____

_____

_____

Name _____

Choose the correct answer.

81. The executive branch checks the legislative branch by:
    A. power to veto bills
    B. power to change laws
    C. power to begin impeachment hearings against legislators
    D. power to set congressional salaries

82. The legislative branch checks the executive branch by:
    A. power to over-ride the president's veto
    B. power to approve presidential appointments
    C. power of the House to impeach the president or vice president
    D. all of the above

83. The legislative branch checks the judicial branch by:
    A. the power of the Senate to approve judicial appointments
    B. the power to impeach justices
    C. the power to appoint justices
    D. B and C
    E. A and B

84. The judicial branch checks the legislative branch by:
    A. the power to impeach a congressional representative
    B. the power to veto laws
    C. the power to find laws unconstitutional
    D. the power to set congressional salaries

85. Which phrase begins the Preamble to the Constitution?
    A. "We hold these truths to be self-evident"
    B. "Congress shall make no law respecting an establishment of religion"
    C. "We the people of the United States"
    D. "When, in the course of human events"

86. Which right is NOT protected by the Bill of Rights?
    A. protection from cruel punishments
    B. protection from unreasonable searches
    C. the right to be free from slavery
    D. the right to free speech
    E. the right to worship freely

87. Which court case ended public school segregation?
    A. Brown vs the Board of Education
    B. Board of Education vs Pico
    C. Plessy vs Ferguson
    D. Regents of U Cal vs Bakkee

88. Which of these abolished slavery?
    A. the first amendment
    B. the Preamble to the Constitution
    C. the Declaration of Independence
    D. the Civil Rights Act of 1965
    E. the thirteenth amendment

89. Which of the following is NOT within the powers of the states?
    A. build highways
    B. levy taxes
    C. make laws
    D. coin money

90. Powers shared by the federal and state governments are:
    A. delegated powers
    B. concurrent powers
    C. inherent powers
    D. reserved powers
    E. implied powers

91. According to the 26th amendment of the Constitution,
    A. women have the right to vote
    B. anyone 18 or older has the right to vote
    C. states cannot deny citizens any rights given by the Constitution
    D. sets January 20 as the day the President's and Vice President's terms begin

92. Which of these comes FIRST in the process of a bill becoming a law?
    A. Committees of the House and the Senate vote on the bill
    B. A member of Congress introduces the bill.
    C. Each house of Congress votes on the bill.
    D. The president signs the bill.

What is the location of these events or landmarks? Write the state.

93. Plymouth Rock _____

94. birth of the Constitution _____

95. Statue of Liberty _____

96. George Washington's home _____

Match the correct description with each name.

_____ 97. Geraldine Ferraro

_____ 98. Janet Reno

_____ 99. Harriet Tubman

_____ 100. Sandra Day O'Connor

A. environmental author
B. American native-born queen
C. first female candidate for Vice President
D. first female Attorney General
E. conductor on Underground Railroad
F. first female Supreme Court justice
G. former slave; speaker for women's rights

SCORE: Total Points _____ out of a possible 100 points

Name _____

U.S. Government, Economy, & Citizenship
SKILLS TEST ANSWER KEY

1. A
2. D
3. J
4. H
5. M
6. B
7. AR
8. D
9. P
10. AR
11. D
12. AM
13. B
14. State
15. Interior
16. Defense
17. Commerce
18. Labor
19. Justice
20. F
21. F
22. T
23. F
24. F
25. NO
26. NO
27. YES
28. NO
29. NO
30. YES
31. NO
32. NO
33. YES
34. NO

35. YES
36. NO
37. YES
38. NO
39. NO
40. NO
41. NO
42. NO
43. YES
44. NO
45. FCC
46. IRS
47. INS
48. FEMA
49. DEQ or EPA
50. CIA
51. H
52. B
53. D
54. C
55. J
56. I
57. C
58. C
59. H
60. C
61. SC
62. P
63. S
64. P
65. S
66. P
67. profit
68. investment

69. earned
70. demand
71. interest
72. surcharge
73. competition
74. income tax
75. the Vice President
76. the Speaker of the House
77. the Capitol Building
78. nine
79. the President
80. life, liberty, and the pursuit of happiness
81. A
82. D
83. E
84. C
85. C
86. C
87. A
88. E
89. D
90. B
91. B
92. B
93. Massachusetts
94. Pennsylvania
95. New York
96. Virginia
97. C
98. D
99. E
100. F

Basic Skills/U.S. History 6-8+

ANSWERS

pages 10–11

1. b	8. d	15. c
2. c	9. b	16. b
3. a	10. c	17. a
4. b	11. c	18. c
5. d	12. a	19. a
6. b	13. c	20. c
7. b	14. a	21. a

page 12

1. colonists, and/or we, the citizens of US
2. Colonists want to break ties with Great Britain
3. A decent respect to the opinions of mankind requires that they should declare the causes which impel them to the separation
4. All people and their opinions matter
5. Natural rights that every human being is entitled to
6. Life, liberty, and the pursuit of happiness
7. To keep our "natural" rights safe and secure for us
8. The people who are governed give them the powers to protect their natural rights
9. To alter or abolish the government and institute a new one
10. When a government becomes destructive to their natural rights.

page 13

Each group should be colored the same color:
Preamble:
- We the people of the United States, in order to form a more perfect Union, establish justice, insure domestic tranquillity, provide for the common defense, promote the general welfare, and secure the blessing of liberty to ourselves and our posterity, do ordain and establish this Constitution for the United States of America.
- The Introduction to the Constitution
- Similar to beliefs of the Iroquois League of Nations
- Only 52 words long
Articles:
- The main body of the Constitution
- First 3 deal with the separate branches of the government
- Last 4 discuss the powers of the states and procedures for amending the Constitution
Amendments:
- Presently, there are 27
- The final section of the Constitution
- These change the Constitution
- More can be added to the Constitution
Bill of Rights
- Made up of the first ten amendments to

the Constitution
- These provide protection for citizens' basic rights & freedoms
- In the beginning, the states insisted that this be added to the Constitution
- The first one protects freedom of speech, thought, and belief (this item may also be grouped as a feature under "Amendments").

pages 14–15

1. A	7. A	13. AM
2. P	8. A	14. A
3. A	9. A	15. B
4. B	10. B	16. A
5. A	11. A	17. A
6. A	12. AM	18. A

pages 16–17

Answers from left to right in each box:

A. 4	G. 9	M. 4
B. 1	H. 1	N. 2
C. 6	I. 1	O. 5
D. 7	J. 6	P. 8
E. 6	K. 5	Q. 3
F. 10	L. 8	

page 18

A. 22	E. 16	I. 20
B. 19	F. 25	J. 13
C. 14	G. 26	K. 15
D. 24	H. 27	L. 14

page 19

1. black arrow from executive branch to legislative branch
2. black circle around Congress or Legislative Branch
3. Legislative Branch colored green
4. Judicial Branch colored red
5. Executive Branch colored brown
6. red arrow from executive branch to legislative branch
7. green arrow from executive branch to legislative branch—to the Senate
8. blue arrow from executive branch to legislative branch—to the Senate
9. orange circle around House of Representatives
10. yellow circle around Senate
11. purple circle around House of Representatives

page 20

A. HIGHLY QUALIFIED: U.S. President (or Chief Executive)
B. APPLICATIONS REQUESTED: Representative
C. LIFETIME JOB: Judge or Chief Justice
D. ARE YOU THE ONE? Senator

1. The Vice-President of the U.S.
2. The Speaker of the House of Representatives
3. President pro tempore of the U.S. Senate

page 21

These are general descriptions of the information students may include.
A. As Commander in Chief of the U.S. armed forces, the President is the top military person in the U.S. Decisions regarding the armed forces are his/her responsibility. He/she can also call in the National Guard from individual states.
B. As Chief Executive, the President chooses people to do the jobs of running the country, and is responsible to see that those people are doing their jobs correctly.
C. As Chief of State, the President is in charge of foreign relations, represents the U.S. to foreign nations, and hosts foreign dignitaries who visit the U.S. The President can also make treaties with other countries.
D. As Chief Legislator, the president can suggest certain laws to Congress. He/she can also veto laws.
E. As Chief of his or her political party, he or she makes decisions about his or her own political party.

page 22

1. Secretary of State
2. Secretary of the Treasury
3. Secretary of Defense
4. Attorney General
5. Secretary of the Interior
6. Secretary of Agriculture
7. Secretary of Commerce
8. Secretary of Labor
9. Secretary of Health & Human Services
10. Secretary of Housing & Urban Development
11. Secretary of Transportation
12. Secretary of Energy
13. Secretary of Education
14. Secretary of Veteran's Affairs

page 23

1. NASA: National Aeronautic Space Administration (oversees space research)
2. IRS: Internal Revenue Service (collects taxes)
3. VA: Veteran's Administration (helps those who served in the Armed Forces)
4. FBI: Federal Bureau of Investigation (gets the facts for crimes against U.S government)
5. CIA: Central Intelligence Agency (international clue gathering)

6. FHA: Federal Highway Administration (plans and builds interstate highways)
7. OSHA: Occupational Safety and Health Administration (sets safety and health standards for working conditions)
8. INS: Immigration & Naturalization Service (oversees immigrants into U.S & who becomes citizens)
9. BIA: Bureau of Indian Affairs (oversees matters having to do with native Americans)
10. BLM: Bureau of Land Management (oversees national lands)
11. NPS: National Park Service (manages national parks)
12. DEQ: Department of Environmental Quality (oversees environmental clean-up)
13. NOAA: National Oceanic and Atmospheric Administration (forecasts weather)
14. FDA: Food and Drug Administration (maintains and regulates quality and safety in food and drugs)
15. FCC: Federal Communications Commission (licenses radio and television—TV, radio signals)
16. FAA: Federal Aviation Administration (ensures safety in airports and on aircraft)
17. FDIC: Federal Deposit Insurance Corporation (insures the money deposited in banks)
18. FTC: Federal Trade Commission (regulates trade & commerce)

pages 24- 25

For the Senate, a red line must connect these (not necessarily in this order):
• 100 members
• Each state has two
• Elected for a six-year term
• Every two years, one-third of body is up for re-election
• Must be at least 30 years old.
• Must be a citizen of the U.S. for at least nine years
• Presiding officer is the Vice-President of U.S.
• President pro tempore presides if vice-president is absent
• Acts as jury in an impeachment process

For the House of Representatives, a blue line must connect these (not necessarily in this order):
• 435 members
• Number of members depends upon size of the state
• 1 representative per 500,000 people in a state
• Has sole power to begin impeachment proceedings
• Elected for two-year term

• Must be at least 25 years old
• Must be re-elected every two years to stay in office
• Presiding officer is the Speaker of the House.
• Must be a citizen of the U.S. for at least seven years
• Only branch that can introduce bills to raise money

page 26

1. representative
2. majority
3. minority
4. Congress
5. odd-numbered
6. Capitol
7. rules
8. expel
9. Congressional Record
10. privileges
11. quorum
12. adjourn
13. U.S. Government
14. terms; two; recess
15. laws

page 27

1. T
2. T
3. T
4. F—It gives Congress the power "to make all laws that are necessary and proper" to carry out its responsibilities.
5. F—"Habeas corpus" means a person's right to appear in court. It's for living citizens.
6. T
7. F—It is a law that punishes people for something they did that was not a crime when they did it.
8. F—These are powers of Congress
9. F—They cannot do either.
10. F—These are powers given to the state government.
11. T
12. F—These are state powers.

pages 28-29

Correct order for steps:

1. F	5. B	9. J	13. A
2. E	6. I	10. D	
3. G	7. K	11. L	
4. C	8. H	12. M	

Footnote: money (revenue) bills

page 30

Corrected statements should be similar to these:
1. The second major body of the Judicial Branch is the Appeals Court.
2. Court justices need much legal knowledge and expertise.
3. The Supreme Court has the power to define the powers of Congress.
4. Supreme Court justices are appointed by the president and approved by the House of Representatives.
5. There are now women serving on the Supreme Court.

6. The Judicial Branch interprets laws. OR The Legislative Branch passes laws.
7. A Supreme Court Justice serves for life.
8. The Constitution did describe the duties of the Supreme Court.
9. It is the executive branch's (or president's) job to enforce laws. OR It is the courts' job to interpret laws.
10. The Constitution left it up to Congress to determine the number of lower courts in the system.
11. The Court is (or is always) allowed to interpret the Constitution.
12. The Supreme Court Building is found in Washington, D.C.
13. There are now 9 Supreme Court Justices.
14. There are two kinds of lower federal courts—district and appellate courts.
15. The appellate court is not different from the appeals court.
16. Once appointed, a Supreme Court justice can be removed (for committing a crime, or if unable to perform duties).
17. Federal Courts have the responsibility to hear all cases involving the laws and treaties of the U.S., including those involving two or more states.
18. Five or more justices must agree before an opinion becomes the Court's official decision.
19. The courts of the judicial system include federal courts and state courts.
20. By law, most people who lose their case in court have a right to appeal to a higher court.

page 31

1. f — Miranda vs Arizona
2. g — U.S. vs Nixon
3. i — Brown vs Board of Education
4. k — Texas vs Johnson
5. b — Plessy vs Ferguson
6. e — Marbury vs Madison
7. c — Engel vs Vitale
8. a — Dred Scott vs Sanford
9. d — Roe vs Wade
10. h — Board of Ed vs Pico
11. j — Regents of U Cal vs Bakkee

page 32

Delegated Powers:
Declare war
Maintain armed forces
Regulate interstate and foreign trade
Admit new states
Establish post offices
Set standard weights and measures
Coin money
Establish foreign policy
Make all laws necessary and proper for carrying our delegated powers

Reserve Powers:
Establish and maintain schools
Establish local governments
Conduct elections
Create corporation laws
Regulate business within the state
Make marriage laws
Provide for public safety
Assume other powers not delegated to the national government or prohibited to states

Shared Powers:
Maintain law and order
Levy taxes
Borrow money
Charter banks
Establish courts
Provide for public welfare

page 33

Questions that students write should be similar to these given below, but may not be precisely the same.

1. the 15th Amendment
(What amendment gave all American men the right to vote, but was not enough to ensure it? It was ratified in 1870.)
2. the 26th Amendment
(What amendment was passed in 1971 and declared that all citizens over 18 could vote?)
3. the 1965 Voting Rights Act
(What act allowed the federal government to keep states from using literacy tests and other practices to discriminate against African-Americans in elections?
4. the "Motor-Voter" Bill
(What bill, passed in 1993, requires states to allow citizens to register to vote when they apply for a driver's license?)
5. the19th Amendment
(What amendment, passed in 1920, gave women the right to vote?)
6. literacy tests and poll taxes
(What are illegal and discriminating tests and taxes that discriminated against African-Americans' right to vote before the Voting Rights Act of 1965?)
7. the electoral vote
(What are the votes called that are cast by the Electoral College that determine a presidential election outcome?)
8. representative democracy
(What is the system of democracy where citizens do not directly make government decisions, but elect officials to govern for them?)
9. a primary election
(What is an election called that chooses a political party's candidate for office?)

10. a campaign
(What name is given to the time of intense activity before an election when candidates present their views and seek voter support?)
11. Republican & Democrat
(What are the two major political parties in our current two-party system?)
12. Elizabeth Cady Stanton, Carrie Chapman, and Lucretia Mott
(Who are three women leaders in the Women's Suffrage Movement?)

pages 34-35

1. residency	9. popular
2. democracy	10. primary
3. Constitution	11. referendum
4. election	12. polling place
5. candidates	13. register
6. ballot	14. turnout
7. platform	15. district
8. political party	16. absentee

pages 36-37

1. Bill Clinton	15. Woodrow Wilson
2. John Adams	16. Thomas Jefferson
3. Herbert Hoover	17. Andrew Jackson
4. John Q. Adams	18. harry Truman
5. Franklin D. Roosevelt	19. Dwight D. Eisenhower
6. James Polk	20. John F. Kennedy
7. Lyndon Johnson	21. Lyndon Johnson
8. Zachary Taylor	22. Richard Nixon
9. Jimmy Carter	23. Theodore Roosevelt
10. Andrew Johnson	24. Abraham Lincoln
11. Ronald Reagan	25. George Bush
12. William McKinley	
13. William Taft	
14. George Washington	

pages 38-39

Answers will vary. Check to see that the student has thoughtfully described each word or symbol in a way that shows some understanding of its meaning.

pages 40-41

Check to see that student maps show red numbers in these places.

1. Philadelphia	12. Florida
2. Georgia	13. Hawaii
3. Virginia	14. Oregon
4. New York City	15. Montana
5. Wyoming	16. Washington
6. Pennsylvania	17. California
7. South Dakota	18. Massachusetts
8. Arizona	19. Alabama
9. Illinois	20. South Carolina
10. Texas	21. Missouri
11. Alaska	

page 42

Answers will vary according to location. Check to see that student has completed activity with accuracy for your community and state.

page 43

Answers will vary. Check to see that student has completed activity with an attempt at thoughtful, personal answers.

pages 44–45

1. Harriet Tubman	9. Janet Reno
2. Soujourner Truth	10. Sandra Day O'Connor
3. Sacajawea	11. Liliukalani
4. Sarah Winnemucca	12. Betty Friedan
5. Geraldine Ferraro	13. Coretta Scott
6. Mother Jones	14. Eleanor Roosevelt
7. Rosa Parks	15. Rachel Carson
8. Mary McLeod Bethune	16. Jane Addams

page 46

1. bank	C. paper
2. twelve	D. money
3. Washington, D.C.	E. checking
4. controls	F. buys, sells (or sells and buys)
A. supervises	G. checks
B. credit	

page 47

1. I	5. L	9. C
2. F	6. B	10. J
3. E	7. M	
4. A	8. H	

pages 48–49

ACROSS	DOWN
1. imports	1. inflation
3. recession	2. supply
4. welfare	5. consumer
6. competition	7. resources
7. risk	9. investment
8. loss	10. unemployed
11. debt	12. expansion
13. interest	14. private
15. saving	16. producer
17. entrepreneur	17. exempt
18. demand	21. rate
19. public	
20. credit	
22. profit	
23. depression	

page 50

1. T	6. F	11. F
2. T	7. F	12. F
3. F	8. F	13. T
4. T	9. T	
5. F	10 T.	